DEFEAT DYSLEXIA!

First Edition

ISBN: 1530552206
ISBN-13: 978-1530552207

www.defeat-dyslexia.com

DEFEAT DYSLEXIA!

THE PARENTS' GUIDE TO UNDERSTANDING YOUR CHILD'S DYSLEXIA

HOLLY SWINTON AND NICOLA MARTIN

Notes on language

In general, it is more sensitive to talk about 'individuals with dyslexia', rather than 'dyslexic people', because dyslexia is far from our only defining characteristic.

However, for the sake of readability, I have opted to use the more straightforward term 'dyslexic person' or simply 'dyslexic'. Personally, I wear this badge proudly: I'm a teacher, an author, a mum – and also a dyslexic.

This book is written in British English.

'He' and 'she' are used in alternating chapters as the generic pronoun.

Notes on formatting

In order to create a friendly reading experience for dyslexics, who often struggle with bright, white paper and small-sized, serif fonts, this book is printed on cream-coloured paper, and formatted using a larger-than-average, sans serif typeface.

CONTENTS

Introduction

Most people know dyslexia as a difficulty with reading, writing and spelling. However, dyslexia traits can also affect other areas of a child's life: how he learns maths or a musical instrument, which sports she enjoys, how his memory functions, how she organises her time. Because dyslexic brains are wired differently, dyslexia even affects how he or she looks at the world.

As a dyslexia specialist, I understand that, for many parents, dyslexia can feel like a demon that's holding their child back from making good progress. That's only part of the story, though. There are positives to dyslexia, not just negatives. Using this book, you'll be able to help your child to defeat the demons of dyslexia – and embrace the best of what it means to be dyslexic.

About the author

So who exactly is writing this book and why should you care what I have to say?

Well, I (Holly Swinton) am a qualified teacher with many years' experience tutoring children with dyslexia. I'm the founder of a local support group for parents of dyslexic children, Dyslexia Midlands, and I'm currently finalising my qualification as a Specialist Assessor in dyslexia with AMBDA (Associate Member of the British Dyslexia Association) status. I regularly give speaking appearances and organise workshops on dyslexia, and I'm often called on to be a media commentator.

What's more, as many of my students are surprised to learn, I'm dyslexic myself. This means I understand how it feels to have dyslexia. It's a big part of why I have such a strong drive to equip parents with the tools to support their dyslexic children. You can read my dyslexia story – and learn how invaluable my parents' support was in helping me to succeed – in the Appendix.

To write this book, I collaborated with Nicola Martin, a non-dyslexic writer, who, like me, was exasperated by the lack of easy-to-read books available for parents to learn about this often-misunderstood subject.

About this book

Defeat Dyslexia! is a jargon-free guide to understanding the full scope of dyslexia. It also contains the vital first steps you'll need to take to support your dyslexic child effectively.

For parents who are unsure whether their child is dyslexic, this book aims to provide clues – ones that are easy to spot and ones that may be hidden. For parents of a diagnosed dyslexic child, this book offers practical advice that will help your child to shine, in school and in life.

Although I have drawn on my own personal experiences of teaching dyslexic children in order to compile this book, I also carried out an in-depth study of the field of dyslexia. This means that the book reflects the latest academic thinking on dyslexia. (The Notes section contains a list of sources.) However, this is not an academic book. Some of the more complex theories have been simplified.

As you'll already have noticed, *Defeat Dyslexia!* is aimed primarily at parents – a fact that is reflected in the language. Grandparents, uncles, aunts, family friends and carers, I know you have a huge impact, too! I hope you'll forgive me for using 'parents' as the generic term. If they choose, young people and adults with dyslexia can also use this book to learn more about dyslexia and how to deal with it more effectively.

The author of this book is British. This means that, for readers outside the UK, some material (on the school system and allowances in exams, for example) will not be directly relevant. However, dyslexia doesn't recognise borders, so I hope that *Defeat Dyslexia!* will help parents from all countries to better understand and support their child's needs.

Every dyslexic is different!

The most important thing to bear in mind while reading this book is that dyslexia looks different in every child. I hope that the case studies I've included – fictionalised accounts of real children with dyslexia – will help to make this clear.

Some dyslexics are naturally good with words, so their dyslexia is most obvious in their maths work. Some dyslexics have problems with text that seems to move on the page, while others have perfect vision, but still struggle to read for other reasons. Some dyslexics mask their dyslexia by working twenty times harder than their peers. There is no 'textbook' dyslexic child. However, parents of dyslexic children are likely to recognise many (if not all) of the dyslexia traits described in this book.

Magical cure?

Finally, if you're looking for a magical cure for dyslexia, this is the wrong book for you. Fix-it-quick programmes are undeniably tempting, but they simply don't work. Dyslexia is too complex, too multi-faceted, to be 'fixed'.

More importantly, it's not a horrific condition that should be 'cured', anyway! It's simply a different way of learning, which needs to be understood and supported. Armed with the practical strategies in this book, every parent has the ability to help their dyslexic child to succeed.

1.

MYTHS AND FACTS ABOUT DYSLEXIA

❝

'My greatest asset is my dyslexia.'

— **BENJAMIN ZEPHANIAH (dyslexic poet)**

Voted one of the nation's favourite poets of all time in a BBC poll

THERE'S SO MUCH CHATTER IN THE MEDIA ABOUT DYSLEXIA THAT it can be hard to know what's real and what's just a myth. Let's start by clearing the air and separating fact from fiction.

MYTH: Dyslexia is 'middle class for stupid'.
FACT: Dyslexics just learn differently.
Dyslexia shouldn't be seen as an 'excuse'. It's a recognised learning difficulty which affects children of all abilities. Dyslexics come in all shapes and sizes, from all walks of life.

MYTH: You can't be dyslexic unless the words move around on the page.
FACT: Dyslexia shows itself in lots of different ways.
Some dyslexics *do* find that the words move, blur or swirl on the page – but many other dyslexics do not have this problem. The simple fact is: there's no single way to spot dyslexia. This is because every dyslexic person has different strengths and weaknesses.

MYTH: If you can read, you can't be dyslexic.
FACT: Different dyslexics have problems with different areas of learning.
Dyslexia is most commonly diagnosed when a child has a problem learning to read. However, dyslexia is not *just* a 'reading disability'. Many dyslexics successfully learn to read, but they struggle in other areas of learning, such as telling the time or mastering multiplication tables. Some dyslexics even use coping strategies that cover up how much they struggle. A dyslexic child might spend ages practising, so that it looks like he can read aloud easily.

MYTH: Dyslexics think backwards.

FACT: Some dyslexics struggle with sequence and direction.

A dyslexic child might read 'dog' as 'god'. He might write 'b' instead of 'd'. He might even put his clothes on backwards! But it's not because he's 'thinking backwards'. He's just having trouble with direction (what's left and right; what's up and down) and sequence (what comes first, second, and third).

Making reversals (muddling up letters and saying words backwards) is just one part of dyslexia. But it's not the *only* part of dyslexia. And some dyslexic children don't make these reversals at all.

MYTH: All left-handed people are dyslexic.

FACT: Dyslexics may be left-handed, right-handed ... or ambidextrous!

When the experts were just starting to figure out dyslexia, a popular theory was that dyslexia had something to do with being left-handed. Lots of studies were carried out, but there has never been enough evidence to prove that dyslexia and being a lefty go (*ahem*) hand-in-hand.

What we do know, though, is that children with mixed dominance or dyspraxia (a condition linked to dyslexia) may not 'choose' a hand until later than other children.

They're more likely to chop and change, swapping hands for different tasks. But don't go assuming a child is dyslexic or dyspraxic, just because he's left-handed!

MYTH: Dyslexia is a new fad.
FACT: Dyslexia has been around forever.
People have always struggled with what we now call dyslexia. The word itself might be new, but the traits of dyslexia are as old as time. Experts are just now looking at the work of historical figures like Leonardo da Vinci and thinking, *'Huh, this guy was probably dyslexic!'*

It's only in the last few years that we've been able to label the condition and give dyslexic children real support.

MYTH: Dyslexia is rare.
FACT: Dyslexia is very common.
Because so many people are never diagnosed, we can't know for sure how common dyslexia is. Estimates vary, but the British Dyslexia Association says that one in ten people is dyslexic. That's a handful in every classroom or workplace. Could the person sitting next to you be dyslexic?

MYTH: Boys are more likely to be dyslexic than girls.
FACT: Boys and girls are equally likely to be dyslexic.
It's true that more boys are *diagnosed* with dyslexia, but don't assume your daughter can't be dyslexic. After all,

not every dyslexic child is diagnosed. And we don't know enough about the science behind dyslexia to say for sure that boys are more likely to be dyslexic than girls. We have to consider the different ways in which boys and girls are expected to behave. It could be that girls are more likely to 'suffer in silence'.

MYTH: Dyslexia only exists in the Western world.
FACT: Rates of dyslexia are similar across the world.
Research has found that incidences of dyslexia are broadly the same around the world. There may be fewer diagnoses in some countries, but (as already discussed) this doesn't mean that dyslexia is less common. Some languages, such as Spanish, are easier for dyslexic children to learn, due to their logical reading and spelling rules. But Spanish children will still experience many of the same difficulties as children in the UK, China, Russia, or anywhere else.

MYTH: You can't remember anything if you're dyslexic.
FACT: Dyslexics struggle with working memory.
Dyslexics don't have what you or I would think of as a 'bad memory'. In fact, some dyslexics naturally have very strong long-term memories. However, most dyslexics have problems processing information using 'working' memory, which is an element of short-term memory. This

means they may come across as less 'on the ball' than their non-dyslexic peers. (Find out more in *Chapter 5: Reading.*)

MYTH: Dyslexics are just lazy.

FACT: Dyslexics have to work harder than everyone else to do many simple things.

It's unfortunate, but dyslexic weaknesses can give the impression of laziness or dreaminess. For example, a dyslexic child may struggle to hold more than one thing in his working memory. This means he may forget a teacher's first two instructions and just remember the last thing the teacher said. This can look like inattentiveness, when really it's not.

In fact, due to their dyslexic weaknesses, children with dyslexia tend to spend much more time and energy on schoolwork than the non-dyslexic children around them. Call that lazy?

MYTH: Dyslexia can't be diagnosed until the age of seven.

FACT: Even small children can show signs of dyslexia.

Most professionals won't formally diagnose until a child is seven, but many agree that dyslexia can be identified at the age of four or five. If a child has related dyspraxia symptoms, it's possible to spot dyslexia even earlier, due to clues in the way he moves. (Find out more in *Chapter 10: Movement.*)

MYTH: The school/the optician will test for dyslexia.
FACT: Most teachers and opticians are not trained to spot dyslexia.

In current teacher training, almost nothing is taught about dyslexia. So how would a teacher know anything more than Joe Public? For this reason, you can't assume a teacher will pick up on the signs of dyslexia. With limited resources to support children with learning difficulties, dyslexics often slip through the cracks of the school system.

As for opticians, the causes of 'visual distortion' (words on the page moving, blurring or swirling) won't be picked up during the basic eye exam that's covered by the NHS. Only some optometrists understand dyslexia. And even those who do will need to carry out further testing to see if a child has the type of visual distortion that's linked to dyslexia. (Find out more in *Chapter 4: Seeing*.)

MYTH: You can't be a doctor if you're dyslexic.
FACT: Dyslexics can do any job they choose.

Doctor, teacher, writer, even astronaut – there's no career path that's off limits to a dyslexic. With the right support, dyslexics can overcome their learning difficulties to aim for the job they want. In fact, dyslexics' special problem-solving abilities can often give them an edge over the rest of the population. (Find out more in *Chapter 14: Problem Solving.*)

MYTH: **If you're dyslexic, you won't amount to anything.**

FACT: **There are successful dyslexics all around you.**

Dyslexics are just a waste of space? Tell that to Richard Branson! The billionaire businessman is just one famous person with dyslexia. Chef Jamie Oliver, actor Whoopi Goldberg, Nobel laureate Carol Greider, and even Prince Harry have all spoken out about their dyslexia.

MYTH: **Dyslexia is something you grow out of.**

FACT: **Dyslexia stays with you for your whole life.**

Dyslexia isn't something you grow out of, but most dyslexics learn to cope with it better as they get older. School – where you have to spend every day reading and writing – can be the hardest time of life for people with dyslexia.

As soon as a dyslexic person leaves school, his dyslexia might feel less glaringly obvious. With the new freedom of being an adult, most dyslexics will choose a job that suits their strengths, rather than magnifying their dyslexic weaknesses. However, it's wrong to think that dyslexia is something you 'just get over', given enough time.

MYTH: **Eighteen is too old to start overcoming dyslexia.**

FACT: **You're never too old to learn how to manage dyslexia.**

Many adult dyslexics feel that, because they didn't receive special support as children, it's 'too late' for them. If they can't tell the time, spell, do maths, or even read by the time they reach adulthood, they assume they're too old to fix the problem. In fact, it's never too late! The same strategies that children use to overcome dyslexia can also be used by adults.

MYTH: Dyslexia is caused by neglect, a mental defect or bad teaching.
FACT: Dyslexia runs in families – it's not 'caused' by anything.
Dyslexia isn't a defect. And it's not caused by parents or teachers 'doing something wrong'. It's just a learning difficulty that's carried in the genes – simple as that!

MYTH: Scientists are close to finding a cure for dyslexia.
FACT: Dyslexia is a combination of difficulties and abilities that needs support, not a 'cure'.
Dyslexia spans such a wide range of learning difficulties that it's unlikely that a pill (or a computer program or a fix-it-quick course) could ever 'cure' it. So be wary of expensive solutions that sound too good to be true!

Scientists have looked for a 'gene for dyslexia' and found that it's not as simple as that. A combination of genetic effects on biochemistry probably causes dyslexia.

It's complicated stuff and even further research is not likely to result in a 'magic solution'. The good news is: we don't need a cure! Any dyslexic can thrive, as long as he's supported in the right way.

2.

DYSLEXIA CHECKLIST

CHECKLISTS OF COMMON SIGNS ASSOCIATED WITH DYSLEXIA can give a rough idea of whether dyslexia may be the root cause of a child's learning difficulties.

Don't expect a dyslexic child to answer 'yes' to every single checklist item, though. After all, every dyslexic child has different strengths and weaknesses. And a fifteen-year-old dyslexic will behave very differently from how she did at seven, so look more for a mismatch between her abilities and those of her peers.

Also remember that your child may have built up strategies or 'work-arounds', which can mask dyslexia. However, if the answer to more than 25 of the questions on this checklist is 'yes', there is a chance your child could be dyslexic.

Reading

Does your child ...

- o rub his eyes after reading for a short time?
- o lean on his hand, covering one eye, while reading?
- o refuse to read long books or ones with small text?
- o frequently lose his place when reading?
- o enjoy being read to, but avoids reading alone?
- o get easily frustrated when reading?
- o guess at what words on the page say, instead of reading them?
- o make mistakes when reading little words (e.g. 'the' or 'an')?
- o read a page of a book, but then has little or no idea what the story is about?
- o read and re-read the same paragraph to understand it?
- o add words into sentences when he's reading, or miss words out?
- o read more slowly than classmates of similar ability?
- o hate reading aloud?
- o find reading comprehension exercises difficult?
- o often read a word correctly and then, further down the page, read the same word incorrectly?
- o read some long, complicated words correctly, but misread some short, easy words?

Writing

Does your child ...

- use mostly phonetic spellings (at an age when her classmates don't)? (*Typically applies to primary-school-aged children only.*)
- spell the same word two or three different ways on a single page?
- jumble up letters within a word (e.g. 'siad' for 'said')?
- occasionally write words from right-to-left, instead of left-to-right (e.g. 'saw' for 'was')? (*Typically applies to primary-school-aged children only.*)
- form some letters back-to-front? (*Typically applies to primary-school-aged children only.*)
- use a mixture of small letters and capitals (e.g. use a capital letter in the middle of a word)?
- find it hard to use a dictionary?
- use only simple words that she can spell?
- make many more spelling errors in written work than in spelling tests?
- mix up spellings of words that sound the same (e.g. 'hear'/'here', 'would'/'wood')?
- use apostrophes in her writing, but balance the apostrophe over a random letter?

- write intelligent responses, which include lots of spelling errors?
- find it hard to put her great ideas down on paper?
- write exam or homework answers that don't answer the question?
- find it hard to get started on her written work?
- structure her written work very poorly, often writing the same thing over and over?
- go off on tangents and use non sequiturs in her written work?
- refuse to check her work when asked (or only pretend to check her work)?
- have very scruffy handwriting?
- regularly get told to hurry up with her written work?
- find it hard, following a break, to remember what she was writing?
- write as little as she can get away with?
- use spellings that suggest she doesn't hear words quite right (e.g. 'massif' for 'massive')?
- have trouble writing in a straight line, even on lined paper?
- use punctuation in the wrong places, or miss it out completely?
- make errors when she copies writing from the whiteboard or textbook?

Speaking

Does your child ...

- often mispronounce words that contain 'f', 'th' or 'v'?
- call objects 'thingamy' or 'whatsit', because he can't remember the right word?
- substitute a similar but wrong word for the one he means (e.g. 'doorstep' instead of 'doormat')?
- ramble on and on when answering a question?
- shout out answers in a group?
- interrupt during conversations?
- jumble up the order of sounds in words (e.g. 'aminal' for 'animal')?
- often trail off in the middle of a sentence?
- struggle to give quick answers to questions?

Maths

Does your child ...

- have trouble with times tables?
- use pen and paper, or count on her fingers, to work out simple maths problems?
- mix up similar symbols, like + and x?
- make mistakes with simple addition?
- write numbers back-to-front or upside-down? (*Typically applies to primary-school-aged children only.*)

- forget the names of maths symbols (e.g. 'divide')?
- often make mistakes when reading or writing down long numbers?
- learn a maths skill, but then can't remember it a week later?
- do far better in classwork than in maths tests?
- find sequences difficult?
- muddle up or misremember methods for adding, subtracting, multiplying, and dividing?
- set out her maths work untidily?

Everyday life

Does your child ...

- often misdial telephone numbers?
- have a history of walking before he could crawl?
- often drop things or trip over?
- have haphazard handwriting?
- grip his pen in a way that seems strange or uncomfortable?
- find it hard to sit still (especially when cross-legged on the floor)?
- often get left and right mixed up?
- eat his meals messily?
- often do up the buttons on his clothing wrong?

- get lost frequently?
- find it hard to tell the time?
- always arrive late?
- find it difficult to recite the months of the year backwards?
- fail to remember homework assignments?
- struggle to remember a list of instructions?
- go upstairs when told to do something and then come down having forgotten why he was up there?
- repeat something over and over to himself, in order to remember it?
- prefer to jot down important information, rather than keep it in his head?
- ask unusual questions?
- come up with outside-the-box solutions to problems?
- have amazing design ability?
- get distracted easily?
- get called 'lazy' or 'sloppy'?
- often joke that he's stupid?

3.

DYS-*WHAT*-IA?:

A QUICK GUIDE TO KEY TERMS

THERE ARE A RANGE OF DIFFERENT TERMS USED WHEN TALKING about dyslexia, and this can cause confusion. 'Specific learning difficulties' (SpLD) is an umbrella term that refers to dyslexia, dyspraxia, dyscalculia, and sometimes ADHD (Attention Deficit and Hyperactivity Disorder) and ASD (Autism Spectrum Disorder). These learning difficulties are *specific*, because they only affect certain areas of learning, as opposed to generalised learning difficulties, such as Down's syndrome. But parents may wonder, what are dyspraxia and dyscalculia? And where do ADHD and autism fit in?

Dyspraxia: difficulty with movement

Dyspraxia (also called Developmental Coordination Disorder or DCD) affects a child's coordination. Both her gross motor skills (used for walking, running, playing sports) and fine motor skills (used for handwriting, cutting, tying shoelaces) can be impaired.

For a dyspraxic child, it's not that there's a problem with the muscles. It's just that the body and the brain struggle to communicate. The messages about how to move the body may not be correctly transmitted or received by the brain. At the extreme end of the spectrum, a dyspraxic child might have trouble walking or running 'normally'. At the mild end of the spectrum, a dyspraxic child might just seem clumsier than average. (Find out more in *Chapter 10: Movement*.)

Although clumsiness may be its most obvious indicator, experts now know that dyspraxia affects many other parts of a child's life. Dyspraxia is also linked with disorganisation and poor time management. (Find out more in *Chapter 11: Time and Organisation*.) Some experts even suggest that dyslexic problems with vision and listening should be referred to as dyspraxia.

As a general rule, dyspraxia can be more straightforward to diagnose, because it shows itself physically. A parent sees a child struggle to tie her shoelaces? Alarm bells sound. Could it be dyspraxia?

Dyslexia, on the other hand, is all inside the brain, so it's harder to diagnose. This is why, in the past, dyspraxia traits have been (and sometimes still are) used to diagnose dyslexia.

Dyscalculia: difficulty with counting

Dyscalculia is the new kid on the block in terms of learning difficulties. We know much more about dyslexia and dyspraxia, but when it comes to dyscalculia and why some children struggle with maths, there's a lot left to find out.

Dyscalculia is usually defined as an abnormal development of how the brain copes with numbers. A child with dyscalculia has very poor number sense, making her practically 'number blind'. She won't be able to look at two numbers and tell which one is bigger. She won't be able to look at the number of dots on a dice and say how many there are, without counting them.

Dyscalculia is so 'new' that there's a lot of debate about it. Some experts argue that the term dyscalculia should be applied more broadly, to any child who has serious problems with maths. Other experts argue that dyscalculia is so similar to dyslexia that they should be classed as the same condition. (Read more on this debate in *Chapter 9: Maths*.) Because most dyslexic children also struggle with maths, finding the dividing line between dyslexia and dyscalculia can be tough.

Other related conditions

Some dyslexic children may also have traits from ADHD (Attention Deficit and Hyperactivity Disorder) or ASD (Autism Spectrum Disorder), which can confuse matters even further. ADHD is a condition characterised by impulsivity and distractibility, which can present with or without the restlessness of hyperactivity. Children on the autism spectrum, meanwhile, may have a very literal worldview, intense interest in particular subjects, trouble understanding social cues, and a tendency towards clumsiness or under-/over-sensitivity to certain stimuli.

A child who's easily distracted and anxious about schoolwork could have dyslexia or ADHD – or she could have both. A child who struggles with motor skills and interpreting her body's signals to her brain could have dyspraxia or autism – or both. Specific learning difficulties are far from clear-cut. (Find out more in *Chapter 15: Co-occurring Conditions*.)

Just give me a definition!

In fact, it may surprise you to learn that there's still no definition of dyslexia that everyone agrees on. Experts in the field are still deciding which learning difficulties to include in a definition of dyslexia and which ones to leave out.

Is trouble tying your shoelaces dyspraxia or dyslexia? Is difficulty with your times tables dyscalculia or dyslexia? If the words on the page move, is that dyslexia or dyspraxia? The answer is: no one quite agrees yet!

In some cases, the answer may be obvious. If your child has severe mobility problems (associated with dyspraxia) or 'number blindness' (associated with dyscalculia), it may be useful to seek a diagnosis of dyspraxia or dyscalculia. However, most children under the SpLD umbrella experience a range of difficulties that could be caused by any number of underlying weaknesses – weaknesses that could be dyslexic, dyspraxic or dyscalculic in origin.

The main thing to remember is that, no matter what we call certain learning difficulties, there are lots of easy ways to help your child. So let's start getting to grips with dyslexia and its related conditions!

4.

SEEING

‘My dyslexia's a weird one – sometimes I have really good days at reading, sometimes I read like a five-year-old.'

— **JAMIE OLIVER (dyslexic chef)**

Celebrity chef, who has sold more than 10 million cookbooks

WORDS THAT SEEM TO MOVE ON THE PAGE MIGHT BE THE most widely known sign of dyslexia. As you can imagine, this kind of distortion makes reading a lot harder!

SIGNS OF DYSLEXIA

When reading hurts

For some dyslexic children, reading can be painful – literally. After reading for just a short time, the child's eyes may start to water, burn or itch. He might get headaches when he tries to read.

One of the root problems is his vision. When he looks at a page of text, the words, letters or numbers can seem to move or distort. The words might appear double. They might swirl, blur, flicker, appear washed out, or seem overpowered by the light. For some children, there are 'rivers' on the page, with some words spaced too close together and some words too far apart.

However, a dyslexic child might not be able to describe what he sees. We all just think that what we see is normal, so a child is not likely to say, 'the words are moving!' This can make it hard for parents to work out what's wrong.

In most cases, a child will just refuse to read. If he *has* to read, he'll choose a short book. And, even then, he may rub his eyes a lot or look pained. He may lose his place very easily when reading aloud or copying from the board.

Parents often find that their dyslexic child loves being read to, but he won't read by himself. This gives a clue that it's dyslexia you're dealing with, not just an uninterested reader.

What's confusing for parents is the fact that more than one condition can cause reading to feel painful. Binocular instability and Meares-Irlen Syndrome both have similar symptoms – and both are likely to affect dyslexics. A dyslexic child may have binocular instability or Meares-Irlen Syndrome or a combination of both!

Binocular instability

Binocular instability is where the eyes don't work together as a team. Every time we move our eyes (as we do every few seconds), we have to re-align our eyes, so that they're both focused on the same spot. Children with binocular instability have to work much harder than normal to re-align their eyes.

Binocular instability is a relatively common problem and one that doesn't just affect dyslexics. However, studies have found that people with dyslexia are more likely to suffer from binocular instability.

A tell-tale sign of binocular instability is that a child might cover one eye while he's reading. Many dyslexics do it without realising it. 'I'm just resting my face in my hand while I read,' he might say. *Hmmm*. Or is he also using his hand to cover one eye?

This is called 'patching' and it can feel like a quick fix. Reading using just one eye means that the eyes don't need to work together, so reading may become easier.

Patching might make things easier in the short-term, but it's not a long-term solution. In order to really get the most out of reading, children need to train both of their eyes to work together.

Meares-Irlen Syndrome

A different condition that causes the words to distort on the page is Meares-Irlen Syndrome. Since the 1980s, it's been suggested that the 'glare' of black text on a white background can lead to visual distortion (moving, blurring or swirling words) for some readers.

Helen Irlen, one of the women to discover the syndrome, says that the problem is caused by looking at words under white light – the type of light we get from the sun and conventional light bulbs. (Olive Meares also described the same condition, leading to the term Meares-Irlen Syndrome.) The solution to this problem lies in looking at text through a coloured lens. Many children find that coloured glasses make the words stop moving.

Hand-eye coordination

If a child has distorted vision, it can also affect his depth perception. He may find it hard to judge how far away objects are. As a result, his hand-eye coordination may be poor. All kinds of sports – as well as everyday activities – require the eyes and the hands to work together. Whether it's catching a ball or pouring a cup of tea, poor hand-eye coordination can look like clumsiness.

However, there are other reasons that a dyslexic child may be un-coordinated. Dyspraxia, a condition where the brain and the body don't communicate properly, can overlap with dyslexia, leading to problems with coordination. (Read more in *Chapter 10: Movement*.)

Crucially, it's important to remember that not every dyslexic child suffers with distorted vision. For some children, like Emily (see case study), problems with vision can be a real struggle. But there are many other children, like Rachel (see case study), who don't have any problems with their vision – but they still can't read easily. The next chapter tackles the other issues that a dyslexic child may face when he tries to read.

SEEING – KEY SIGNS OF DYSLEXIA:

- Child finds that the words on the page 'move' or appear distorted
- Suffers headaches or sore eyes after reading for a short time
- Covers one eye while reading
- Enjoys being read to, but is unwilling to read alone
- Problems with hand-eye coordination, including clumsiness
- (Remember: not all dyslexic children have trouble with their vision)

Case study: Emily and the rivers (part 1)

Emily never understood why publishers did such a poor job with their books. Why make the gaps between some words really small, and the gaps between other words really wide? It was weird.

At school, Emily struggled with reading. Instead, during her lessons, she used her pencil to trace the rivers down the page. *Maybe it's a pattern*, she thought. Why else would books be printed that way?

Case study: Duncan and the blue glasses (part 1)

Duncan was always a good student. Oh, maybe he struggled a bit with spelling, but his reading was fine and his teachers weren't worried. His sister was diagnosed with dyslexia, but, because Duncan could read, no one thought to test him.

One day, Duncan was horsing around and he tried on his sister's blue glasses – the ones that helped her to read.

'Mum!' Duncan called out. 'These glasses are amazing. The words have stopped moving. It's so much easier to read now!'

Case study: Rachel and Rachel's mum (part 1)

Rachel's mum was a very smart lady. She liked to know everything about everything, so she buried herself in books. Other mums watched TV, but not Rachel's mum!

Rachel, on the other hand, did *not* like reading. She was inquisitive, but she didn't like school at all.

One day, Rachel got home from school to find that her mum was very excited. 'I know what the problem is!' Rachel's mum said. 'I read all about it in a book! The words on the page move when you try to read, don't they, Rachel?'

Rachel wrinkled her nose. 'No,' she said.

Undeterred, Rachel's mum made Rachel do lots of tests. She grew very frustrated when Rachel kept saying the words on the page didn't blur or swirl or move at all.

'Well!' Rachel's mum said, throwing down the book. 'You can't be dyslexic, then!'

SUPPORTING DYSLEXIA

Visiting a specialist optician

Getting a child tested by an optometrist who understands dyslexia is very important. A basic eye exam (the type covered by the NHS) will *not* usually test for binocular instability or Meares-Irlen Syndrome. In fact, testing for visual distortion can take twice as long as a regular eye exam, which means the optometrist will charge a private fee.

However, if you suspect your child has problems with visual distortion, it's usually worth paying a one-time fee to be certain. Parents should make sure the person they visit is a qualified optometrist, who will check for both conditions. Various organisations offer vision testing for suspected dyslexia, but be aware that many are staffed by people without qualifications.

Eye exercises for binocular instability

If a child is found to have binocular instability, the condition can be treated by doing eye exercises. These exercises help to train the eyes to work better as a team, so that vision becomes less blurry and distorted.

Booklets of exercises for binocular instability are produced by optometrists. These exercises are well-respected. They've been prescribed by optometrists for many years, and they've been proven to work by independent research.

However, parents should be wary of other types of eye exercises that they may be offered to 'cure' dyslexia. Vision training (also called vision therapy) involves eye exercises and may also include use of yoked prisms (which change how you see the world) and computer programs.

Vision training is usually carried out by Behavioural Optometrists, who tend to work outside of regular optometry. A course of vision training can take several months of weekly sessions, so it can be very expensive.

Many parents are satisfied that a course of vision training really helps their dyslexic child. However, there isn't independent research to back up the idea that it works. Parents should, therefore, approach vision training with caution, and seek personal recommendations.

Coloured overlays and glasses

For children with Meares-Irlen Syndrome, reading a page of text through a lens of a certain colour can lessen the symptoms. Coloured overlays are a popular solution. These are sheets of see-through coloured film which can be placed over a page of a book or a sheet of paper. Blue is the most popular colour, but different children need different colours.

For some children with Meares-Irlen Syndrome, coloured overlays aren't enough. In these cases, the answer may be coloured glasses. These glasses, which are completely tailored to a child's needs, have a higher success rate. Even for children who do get some benefit out of overlays, parents may be interested in glasses as a more convenient way for their child to get the same effect. However, coloured glasses can be expensive.

When it comes to both glasses and overlays, it's very important to find exactly the right colour for your child. Some teachers have read a little about the subject and will let a child pick from a handful of different coloured overlays at school. Unfortunately, a coloured overlay of the wrong colour will have no effect at all. Likewise, coloured glasses have to be exactly the right colour for your child's eyes. It's no good just running out and buying a cheap pair of tinted glasses, either!

Indeed, the right shade for coloured glasses is likely to be different from the shade needed for overlays. This is because coloured glasses change the colour of *everything* you see, forcing your brain to change its perception. Overlays only tint the page you're reading, so the overall way you see the world doesn't change.

The Irlen system and the Wilkins system

There are two main types of coloured glasses/overlays available: those that follow the Irlen system and those that follow the Wilkins system. Irlen products and Wilkins products are made using different dyeing processes. The way that testing is carried out to find the right colour is different, too.

Many people report good results from Irlen glasses and overlays (which are available from regional Irlen centres across the UK), but there's more independent research to back up the Wilkins system, so that's what this book will concentrate on.

Under the Wilkins system, a child is tested using a machine called an Intuitive Colorimeter. These machines can be found in certain optometrists' offices. Testing takes about half an hour. It is *not* covered by the NHS.

During testing, the child looks through an opening in the machine at a page of text. The text is lit up by coloured light. The colour of the light can be adjusted to find the exact shade that makes it easiest for the child to read the page of text. The optometrist can then create a prescription for glasses in this specific colour.

In case you're wondering, blue glasses do not make the world turn blue! For most people, everything looks completely normal when they wear coloured glasses. This is because your brain adapts to the coloured lens.

One more thing: the colour specified for the glasses may change over time. The Wilkins system recommends that children are tested once a year on the Intuitive Colorimeter. Adults usually need testing less often.

Cheap and cheerful alternatives

Proper testing is advised if your child suffers from severe visual distortion. However, for parents on a limited budget, see-through coloured folders from stationery shops can sometimes work as 'cheap and cheerful' coloured overlays. Many companies also sell overlays in a range of colours – at a higher cost, of course. Coloured reading rulers (thinner strips of coloured film) and computer overlays are also available.

The problem with opting for a 'cheap and cheerful' fix, however, is that it can be hard to find exactly the right colour overlay for your child's eyes. At best, a close colour match will ease the symptoms of Meares-Irlen Syndrome a bit. At worst, it will have no effect at all. Even if blue is your child's ideal colour, the wrong shade of blue might make the overlay useless.

For children who do a lot of reading on the computer, changing the settings is a quick (and free!) fix that can help to ease the pain of reading. Adjusting the default

Windows background colour (using *Control Panel >
Personalization > Window Color > Advanced Appearance
Settings*) automatically changes the background colour of
Microsoft Word, Microsoft Excel and other documents. It's
a function that's available in most types of computers,
including older models. Alternatively, you can change the
background colour of a Microsoft Word document within
the program itself, by selecting: *Page Layout > Page Color.*

Parents should be aware that computer tweaks and
mass-produced overlays are probably better used as a
temporary stop-gap while investigating more expensive
and precise overlay/glasses solutions. Quick fixes may be
better than nothing, but a completely tailored solution is
likely to be best of all.

Beyond visual distortion

Solutions to visual distortion can seem like an instant fix
for dyslexia. Indeed, finding a way to stop the words on
the page from moving, blurring or swirling can make a
huge difference for children.

However, getting rid of visual distortion won't mean
that your child is suddenly able to read. As I'll discuss in
the next chapter, dyslexic children may struggle to read
for reasons that have nothing to do with how the words on
the page look.

SEEING – KEY SUPPORT FOR DYSLEXIA:

- Visit an optometrist who understands dyslexia
- Eye exercises can help with binocular instability
- Coloured overlays and coloured glasses can help with Meares-Irlen Syndrome
- Testing using the Intuitive Colorimeter will find your child's ideal colour

---

Case study: Emily and the rivers (part 2)

Emily was a teenager before she found out that not everyone saw the rivers that she saw in books.

She visited an optometrist who knew a lot about dyslexia. The optometrist gave Emily eye exercises to help with binocular instability and recommended coloured overlays, as well. Now, for the first time, Emily only sees rivers when she takes her dog on country walks!

Case study: Duncan and the blue glasses (part 2)

Duncan's mum took Duncan for a dyslexia assessment. When Duncan was diagnosed with dyslexia, his mum was very surprised, but the assessor explained that, even though Duncan seemed to be doing well at school, his progress was much slower than it should have been.

Duncan's next stop was an optometrist, to be tested for his *own* pair of coloured glasses. His glasses are a slightly lighter shade of blue than his sister's, and they make reading so much easier.

Case study: Rachel and Rachel's mum (part 2)

Rachel's mum was indeed very smart. But it turned out that, in this case, she was wrong! When Rachel was eventually tested for dyslexia, it emerged that she *was* dyslexic. It's just that her dyslexia didn't include visual distortion.

Luckily, Rachel's mum was able to use all of her book-smart intelligence to begin helping Rachel with her reading, writing, and maths – all the things that made Rachel hate school. Rachel still likes watching TV more than she likes reading books, but she's started to hate school a little bit less.

5.

READING

MANY DYSLEXIC CHILDREN FIND READING DIFFICULT. IT'S often one of the first signs of dyslexia that is noticed by others. Problems with reading can be made worse by the problems with seeing that some dyslexics experience, but it's not *only* words that move on the page which makes it harder than average for a dyslexic child to read.

SIGNS OF DYSLEXIA

The house that dyslexia built

Imagine trying to build a house, but not really understanding *how* to build it. You might muddle through and put some of the right bricks in the right places. But, as soon as you put another layer of bricks on top, everything gets a bit shaky. The foundations are so weak that the more you build of the house, the shakier it becomes.

For many dyslexic children, this is what it feels like when they learn to read at school. They might 'muddle through' and learn how to read some words. In fact, some will muddle all the way through into adulthood, but they'll still be missing those all-important foundations of reading.

Most dyslexic children will struggle with reading to some extent. For many children, their struggles will be obvious. However, others are 'compensating dyslexics', who will muddle through, often very successfully, but ultimately still need support.

A compensating dyslexic *compensates* for her shortcomings by putting in extra time and effort. She might spend hours and hours reading a chapter that should have taken her just thirty minutes. Some compensating dyslexics can fool teachers and parents into thinking they're confident readers: she'll know the most common words on the page and she can guess the rest.

However, as she gets older and the text she's reading becomes harder, the problems of a compensating dyslexic become more noticeable. This is because, for both compensating dyslexics and children whose dyslexia makes reading feel impossible, there are some root problems that need to be addressed.

Struggling to read even simple words

At the extreme end of the spectrum, a dyslexic child might find reading so difficult that she may not be able to read a short, simple word like 'cat'. This is not because she's stupid. It's not because she has no interest in reading. (Dyslexic children usually *love* being read to. They just won't pick up a book and read alone.)

The problem is: she doesn't grasp the *process* of how to read.

Other children pick up the process of reading naturally. They can start to read just by looking at a word and hearing the teacher say it. But, for a dyslexic child, the reading process won't feel natural or easy.

Phonological awareness

To begin learning to read, a child needs good 'phonological

awareness'. This means understanding all the speech sounds that make up the English language and being able to play around with them. (For example, good phonological awareness makes it possible to identify rhyming words and find words that begin with the same sound.)

To read, a child must learn how to break down language into its separate sounds, and then blend those sounds together to make a whole word. Even to read a simple word like 'cat', a child has to learn its individual sounds. Then she has to blend together each of the sounds to get the full word, with the emphasis in the right place.

If a child has good phonological awareness, she can look at a word on the page and 'sound out' each separate speech sound. ('Sounding it out' is a popular teaching method called phonics.) However, a dyslexic child is likely to have poor phonological awareness. She may find it hard to remember all the speech sounds, or she may put those speech sounds in the wrong order.

Mixing up letter symbols

For some children, the problem lies partly with how their eyes and ears work. After all, reading is all about symbols (the words on the page) and sounds (the words we speak). When we read, we decode symbols and convert them into sounds. However, a dyslexic child might have trouble seeing the symbols properly, due to visual distortion. As detailed in *Chapter 4: Seeing*, this immediately puts her at a disadvantage.

What's more, even if she has perfect vision, a dyslexic child might find it hard to link the letter symbols to the sounds. These connections don't tend to stick as easily in her long-term memory. She may mix up similar-looking symbols like 'u' and 'a'. As a result, she'll look at the words 'cup' and 'cap' and think they're the same.

Not hearing the sounds correctly

When it comes to 'sounding out' each word as she reads, a dyslexic child might run into yet more trouble. She may not be able to hear the speech sounds correctly, due to a common dyslexic hearing issue: poor auditory discrimination.

If two speech sounds are very similar, a dyslexic child may struggle to hear the difference between them. So the speech sounds /f/ (*fuh*, as in 'find') and /θ/ (*thuh*, as in 'think') may sound the same to her ears. As a result, she'll be confused when she tries to read the word 'thing', because she's expecting it to begin with an F.

Another important part of learning to read is being able to tell where the spaces between words lie. There is only a subtle pause between the words in a phrase like 'each other', and a dyslexic child is likely to struggle to hear such tiny pauses. Therefore, she may expect to read 'each other' as just one word ('chuther'), not two. (Find out more about auditory discrimination in *Chapter 8: Speaking and Listening*.)

Tripped up by language rules

Even if a dyslexic child is able to master 'sounding it out', a lot of words on the page will still stump her. This is because the English language is filled with words that can't be sounded out. To read these words, children must learn advanced phonics patterns and extra language rules.

For example, 'silent K' is a language rule. The word 'know' can't be sounded out, because it has a silent K. Teachers rarely explain these rules and simply expect children to pick them up automatically. Hear 'know' read out loud enough times and the teacher expects you to, well, *know*.

However, a dyslexic child may find it much harder than average to see these patterns, visualise words, and pick up language rules. Any difficult words (such as ones with silent letters, or ones from foreign languages) may give her grief.

What's also common is that a child may be able to read a word like 'knowledge', because it's visually distinctive and relatively common, but struggle to read a word like 'pivot', because she may not have come across it before and may not have the skills to sound it out.

Memorising words, instead of learning how to read them

At one end of the dyslexic spectrum, there are the children who can't even get started with reading. At the other end of the spectrum, there are the 'muddlers'. These are the children who have successfully muddled through, even though they don't really understand 'sounding it out' or language rules.

One type of 'muddler' might be a child with a very strong long-term memory – maybe even a photographic memory. She'll muddle through reading by memorising words. She'll remember the shape of words she's seen and how to say them.

As a result, she can trick people into thinking she's a good reader. The trouble is, deep down, she's just like the children who can't even read the word 'cat'. She hasn't learned the *process* of how to read. So, if she's given an unknown word, a name, or a nonsense word to read, she panics. She doesn't know how to sound it out. She doesn't know the language rules.

When faced with a new and unknown word, a muddler will simply guess. She will look at the shape of the words and then think of a phrase that might fit those shapes, based on the context of what she's reading. For example:

> **He defiantly stared at it.**
> Dyslexic child reads:
> *He definitely started it.*
>
> **Please make sure you have filed this in the box.**
> Dyslexic child reads:
> *Please make sure you have filled in this box.*

In fact, some dyslexics get so good at guessing unfamiliar words that they come across as confident readers. Other dyslexics are not so good at guessing. To non-dyslexics, their guesses can seem crazy, like the reader is being silly or not trying at all. This is far from the case. She's probably trying twice as hard as her non-dyslexic peers.

Weak working memory

Since dyslexics struggle so much with the process of reading, it's not surprising that they also find reading comprehension difficult. Even when a dyslexic child manages to read the words, she might not get the meaning of the story. An easy way to spot dyslexia is to find out whether a child understands a story when it's read aloud by a parent or teacher. If she can take in its meaning while listening, she's obviously perfectly intelligent. The problem she's having is with the *process* of reading.

Reading comprehension can be tricky for dyslexic children because of working memory issues. But, hold up, what exactly *is* working memory?

Working memory is how we keep track of information, via the short-term memory store. It allows us to remember several pieces of information at once (the digits of a telephone number, for example). Yet working memory is also active. Using working memory, we can manipulate the information in our short-term memory in different ways. We can draw conclusions, solve problems, and make connections.

While reading, a child's working memory is hard at work. It helps her to figure out what's going on in the story, hold on to what's just happened, remember reading rules, and come up with the correct pronunciation of long words. Basically, working memory is the mental equivalent of a piece of scrap paper, covered with doodles and class notes.

However, dyslexics tend to have *weak* working memories. This means a dyslexic child will be able to hold fewer pieces of information in her short-term memory. Like a glass that's almost full of water, her working memory will be easily filled to capacity. It might take more effort for her to solve problems and make connections.

Weak working memory can also make it harder to transfer new skills to long-term memory. Parents often find that their dyslexic child can perform a task when it's uppermost in her mind, but she won't remember how to do it the next day. Even when she does store a skill in her long-term memory, she may find she has problems accessing this memory quickly.

A stressful reading experience

Working memory isn't connected to intelligence. But a strong working memory can make someone *seem* like she's on the ball. And a weak working memory can make someone *seem* like she's scatter-brained. A dyslexic child with a weak working memory will be so busy concentrating on the process of reading that she'll often fail to follow what's going on in the story. So, when the teacher asks her a reading comprehension question, she'll have no idea how to answer it.

Unsurprisingly, dyslexic readers are often *stressed* readers. When your memory's working overtime, it can make reading really stressful. Mastering the process of reading is so much harder for a dyslexic child that it's no wonder she may get easily frustrated by words. However, it's not the case that a dyslexic child can't learn to read. As soon as her problems are understood and supported, the stress of reading will begin to ease.

READING – KEY SIGNS OF DYSLEXIA:

- Child enjoys being read to, but is unwilling to read alone
- Reads a page, but then has no idea what the story is about
- Panics when faced with a new word
- Makes crazy guesses at what a phrase says
- Gets easily frustrated by reading

Case study: Jack and the cat that wouldn't sit on the mat (part 1)

Jack's best friend in the whole world was his cat, Sooty. But, at ten years old, Jack couldn't even read the word 'cat', despite having perfect vision.

For Jack, trying to read was torturously slow – no matter how much helpful meowing Sooty did.

Jack's school thought that he was mentally backward, but his parents knew that their son was bright and inquisitive. He just couldn't read.

Case study: Martha and her big library (part 1)

Martha made a point of reading all the classics. Austen and Eliot and Dickens. She loved words and stories and, more than that, she wanted to prove to everyone that she was a good reader.

Oh, she'd had a bit of trouble with reading when she was really young. But she'd got lots of help from her mum and, since then, she'd developed a good reading age. All of her problems were behind her. Weren't they?

SUPPORTING DYSLEXIA

Going back to basics

The 'house that dyslexia built' will always be shaky, until real foundations are laid. Even if she's muddled through reading for many years, a dyslexic child will still benefit from help in mastering the process of how to read easily and effectively.

The only thing to do, then, is to go right back to the beginning and help your child to learn, in stages, how to pronounce and read words (both real and nonsense ones). The majority of experts now agree that using the dyslexia-friendly 'phonics' method is most effective. Going back to basics can seem overwhelming to parents. However, it's not usually the long process it first appears to be. Once the gaps in her knowledge of reading are filled in, a child can race forward in her progress.

Multi-sensory learning

Helping your child with reading may require adjustments. Don't just do the same old school stuff with her. Parents must stay aware of how their child learns best: her 'learning style'. Consider these three sense-based learning styles:

> **Learning by looking (visual learning)**
> *For a visual learner, it's easier to learn by looking at a spider diagram or watching a live/filmed demonstration.*

Learning by listening (auditory learning)

For an auditory learner, it's easier to listen to someone explain all about a subject, or tie facts to sounds and songs.

Learning by doing (kinaesthetic learning)

For a kinaesthetic learner, it's easier to learn when you move around, use your body, and get physically involved.

Try to figure out which learning style best fits your child. But also be aware that most dyslexic children respond best to 'multi-sensory learning'. That is, types of learning that don't just rely on one sense, but all five senses.

Encourage your child to learn using not just speech and sight, but also touch, taste, smell, movement, and colour. Not only does multi-sensory learning make it easier for new facts to stick in a dyslexic child's mind, it can also make homework time a lot more fun!

What does multi-sensory learning look like in practice? Well, to help a child to master the phonics pattern /ʃ/ (*sh*, as in 'sheep'), the two of you might trace the letters in the air, or in a sand pit, or in the bath. You could use plastic, tactile letters in a particular colour to spell out 'sh' on the table. You could associate the word with an action, such as putting your finger to your lips and saying, 'shh!' like a bossy librarian.

These types of techniques can be especially useful in learning common (but tricky) sight words, such as 'said', 'because', and 'Wednesday'.

The Rule of Ten

A word of warning: due to her weak working memory, a dyslexic child learning to read will need to repeat phonics and reading rules many more times than her classmates. This is where the Rule of Ten comes in. When a dyslexic child is learning to do something, she will need to practise ten times more than a non-dyslexic child. (This may be an oversimplification in some cases, but it is normally a helpful principle.) Although this can mean a lot of repetition, it really is the best way to help your child with her reading.

However, 'repetition' need not mean dreary rote learning (saying something over and over again in the same way). Try and find as many different ways of repeating key facts as possible. Appeal to the senses and make repetition *fun*. Play educational games or puzzles; get crafty with paint or clay or ribbons; make up a song; practise reading rules while kicking a ball or hop-skip-jumping. Schools tend to teach reading in just one way, but that doesn't mean parents have to do the same at home!

Reading for learning ... and for pleasure

When it comes to the nuts and bolts of reading, parents

can use educational, phonics-based reading books to help their child. Some of these consist of a single large book (such as Keda Cowling and Frank Cowling's *Stride Ahead*), offering a comprehensive reading programme. Other book series tell a story, while also highlighting a particular phonics pattern (such as Allan Frewin Jones's *Talisman* series). The *Suggested Further Reading* section contains a full list of recommended phonics-based reading books.

In addition to these 'learning' books, also encourage your child to read books of her own choosing for fun. Many dyslexic children, especially older 'muddlers', will get pleasure out of reading, even though they know they're not reading every word correctly. Think of it in terms of your child practising two different styles of reading: the kind you do in an exam and the kind you do on a beach.

Finding a balance between reading for learning and reading for pleasure is important. Too much of the former and your child will begin to dread reading of any kind. Too much of the latter and she'll stop making progress.

Check the readability of what your child is reading

Always make sure that whatever book your child is reading is at the correct level for her. If it's too hard, she may get frustrated with the book and give up. So check its readability, using one of these quick tests:

Ask her to read a single page aloud and see how many words she struggles with. As a general rule, your child should be able to easily read nine out of every ten words on the page. Alternatively, use the Five Finger Test, where your child opens the book at a random page and reads from the top. When she gets to a word she doesn't know, she puts a finger (or a thumb) on that word and continues reading. If she runs out of fingers and thumbs before she gets to the bottom of the page, it is probably too hard for her to read independently. Find a different book that's on her current reading level. (If she's still desperate to read the harder book, you could offer to read it to her. The object is to reduce her frustration with reading, not to take away a book she's enjoying!)

The tiredness factor

Always remember that reading can feel like a struggle for a dyslexic child. And anything that's a struggle is tiring. For this reason, forcing a dyslexic child to read for a long stretch is frustrating for everyone involved.

One of the best ways to combat 'the tiredness factor' is to read *with* a child, alternating between paragraphs in the style of 'I read, you read'. This creates a pattern: a short period of reading, followed by a short period of rest. While the parent reads aloud, the child gets a little break and is able to relax and follow the story. It is reading little and often that gets the best results.

Make your home a reader's paradise

To encourage your child to read, make sure she has plenty of things *to* read. Stock your home full of reading materials. Not just fiction, but also magazines, non-fiction books, newspapers, print-outs from websites. Look out for anything that ties in with your child's interests and any forthcoming activities. (This might mean reading material about exotic animals, if you're planning a trip to the zoo, for example.) Regularly visit the library with your child, so that she always has a chance to look for new books. Many libraries have holiday reading programmes, which can be a great motivator, and some even have schemes just for dyslexic children.

Make sure your child feels that reading can be fun and informative. Share your own (positive) experiences with reading. Talk about your favourite books. If you learn a new fact from a book or magazine, tell your child. Read out interesting parts of websites or newspapers to your child. If she sees you getting something out of reading, it will make her want to read, too.

Audio books

If your child is a reluctant reader, talking books (on CD or audio file) can be a gateway to reading. They can make a long car journey pass peacefully or take the boredom out of chores. They can also help your child to see that books can be a good thing and inspire her to soldier on with her own reading.

Audio books can be borrowed from the library or downloaded via the Internet. Also try to get hold of a physical copy of the book. While you're listening to the talking book, encourage your child to follow the words with her finger. It may not always be possible to do this, but try to do it for at least a chapter or two.

Quick progress

Once a dyslexic child is supported in the right way, reading is usually the area where she can make the fastest progress. Dyslexics' reading usually improves dramatically once they're no longer drowning in words they don't know.

According to the Oxford English Dictionary, learning just 100 of the most common everyday words can allow you to read 50% of things that you are given. And, armed with 1,000 common words, your child will be able to read 75% of what's put in front of her. What's more, once she gets to grips with the hows and whys of reading, she'll become a much more confident reader – one who's no longer panicked when she's given a new word to read.

READING – KEY SUPPORT FOR DYSLEXIA:

- Make sure the nuts and bolts of language are learned inside-out
- Repeat, repeat, repeat! Appeal to the senses to make sure common sight words stick
- Use educational phonics books to build up reading skills and learn common patterns
- Check your child is reading books that are at the correct level
- Make reading fun, and include regular rest breaks
- Fill your house with reading material
- Share your own positive reading experiences with your child
- Play audio books during car journeys or 'chore time'

Case study: Jack and the cat that wouldn't sit on the mat (part 2)

Jack's parents took him to an Educational Psychologist for tests. The tests proved what they already knew: Jack was of above-average intelligence.

The problem was dyslexia – such severe dyslexia that he hadn't been able to pick up even the basics of reading. Jack was brought 'back to basics' and taught how to sound out words till he really understood them. He was also given books that looked grown-up, but were at the right level for him.

Now, just a few months later, Jack loves to read – especially with Sooty on his lap, purring.

Case study: Martha and her big library (part 2)

Martha's dyslexia was well camouflaged by her intelligence and hard work. She passed her exams and went to university. But, gradually, she began to realise that not everyone read the way that she did.

At university, she realised that not everyone took two hours to read a chapter of a textbook. Not everyone had to re-read every paragraph to understand its meaning.

When Martha's dyslexia was diagnosed, she received a special grant to buy a computer program to read complex books to her, so that she could really focus on their meaning. She was also given extra time in her university exams.

Martha still loves to read the classics – Austen, Eliot, Dickens – but she's no longer doing it to prove anything to anyone.

6.

SPELLING

''

'People with dyslexia often have a great creative ability and a drive and an energy to find inventive solutions for life.'

— **ARI EMANUEL (dyslexic talent agent)**
Co-CEO of one of the biggest talent agencies in the world and the 'real' Ari Gold (Entourage)

SPELLING CAUSES PROBLEMS FOR ALMOST ALL DYSLEXICS. Weak working memory and left/right confusion may leave a dyslexic child making muddled mistakes. And, as he gets older, he's likely to have a 'spelling age' that's years behind his real intellect.

SIGNS OF DYSLEXIA

A common Achilles' heel

Many dyslexics say that spelling is their Achilles' heel (even if they might spell it *Akillees' heal*!). Spelling is what trips them up and stops them from producing good work.

Some dyslexic spelling mistakes are the type of common lapses that everyone makes from time to time. The difference is that dyslexics will make these mistakes almost *all* the time. Other spelling mistakes are particular to dyslexics. These mistakes are rooted in dyslexic problems with sequencing and direction.

Transparent and non-transparent languages

The fact is, we English-speaking spellers don't have it easy. Over the centuries, following hundreds of wars and invasions, English has gradually incorporated words from many other languages. For example, 'chef' is French in origin, while 'chaos' is Greek in origin. The French generally pronounce 'ch' as /ʃ/ (*sh*, as in 'sheep'), but the Greeks pronounce 'ch' with a /k/ sound (*kuh*, as in 'coin').

English also keeps evolving. Back when we used to speak Old English, we pronounced the K in 'know' and 'knight', but now they're silent. 'Chav' is an example of a new, modern word that doesn't follow any of the usual rules. The letter V is traditionally followed by an E, but chavs aren't traditional!

It's all very confusing. This is why we call English an opaque or non-transparent language. English doesn't follow a regular, consistent set of rules. And, often, words aren't spelled the way they are spoken. This makes it difficult for English-speaking dyslexics to confidently spell. By contrast, dyslexics in countries like Spain, which has a transparent language (with fewer non-native words), tend to struggle less with spelling.

Spelling everything phonetically

In English, you can't rely on a word being spelled the same way that it's spoken. Instead, children have to master spelling rules. These rules tell us, for example, that sometimes we should spell words that end in an /ɪ/ sound (*ee*, as in 'sandy') with a Y.

However, a lot of dyslexic children simply never master spelling rules. Instead, they'll doggedly continue to spell words the way they're spoken. As a result, a dyslexic child might produce work that's filled with phonetic ('spell it as you say it') spellings. He'll spell 'said' as *sed*. He won't realise that a /f/ sound (*fuh*, as in 'find') can be produced by the letters 'ph', so he'll continue to spell 'graph' as *graf*, even as his peers 'grow out' of this habit.

Struggles with sound-alikes

Some dyslexic children do manage to progress past

phonetic spellings. They'll often be aware that there's a spelling rule they have to follow, but they won't quite remember it correctly. As a result, a dyslexic speller might spell the same word two or three different ways on the same page. He'll try out 'grath', 'graf' and 'gragh' (for 'graph'), all in the space of a few paragraphs.

Homophones (sound-alike words that are spelled differently) are a particularly tricky area of spelling for dyslexic children. Think about the common homophones 'there', 'their' and 'they're'. A dyslexic child will either pick one spelling and use it all the time, or he'll use a strange mixture of all three spellings ('theire', for example).

Jumbled letters

Another common dyslexia trait is using all (or most) of the right letters in a word, but putting them in the wrong order (e.g. writing 'siad' instead of 'said'). This is because dyslexics have problems with sequencing (putting things in the right order).

Let's imagine a dyslexic child wants to spell 'here'. He remembers that the word has four letters. He remembers that it contains the letters H, E and R, but he can't remember what the other letter is, or in what order the letters go. He remembers there is another vowel, so he ends up with ... *hier*.

It's a long and well-reasoned thought process, proving that he's intelligent. But he's still come up with the wrong spelling, because he's never fully grasped how to correctly spell 'here'.

Complicated words

When it comes to longer words, some dyslexic spellings can look downright bizarre to parents. This is because dyslexic spellers often appear to get 'lost' inside a word. The child might repeat letters within a word, like a stuck record. 'Germinate turns into 'germininate', with the 'in' repeated.

The more complicated the spelling, the more a dyslexic child may struggle. Often, he'll simply panic and write down something that bears little resemblance to the real spelling. Alternatively, a dyslexic child may change his written work, in order to use words he can spell. Instead of using the hard-to-spell word 'eccentric', he'll come up with the word 'weird' ... but he can't spell 'weird', either, so he'll write down 'odd', a word he can spell. This is another way in which dyslexic difficulties can mean schoolwork fails to show the child's true intelligence.

Odd formation of letters

A dyslexic child may also scatter his work with letters that are formed back-to-front. This may include 'hidden' backwards letters, such as an 'o' that is drawn clockwise, rather than anticlockwise. It sounds silly to non-dyslexics, but many dyslexics simply forget how letters are supposed to be formed.

Dyslexic children struggle with direction and telling left from right. (Find out more in *Chapter 10: Movement.*) This means that when a younger child puts pen to paper to form a 'b', he draws a stem, but then forgets which way the letter is supposed to bulge, so he ends up writing 'd' by mistake.

Confusion about direction (which way is left and which way is right) may also lead a dyslexic child to spell some whole words backwards. When he tries to write 'was', it will make it on to the paper as 'saw'. This is particularly common when spelling single words. He simply has a momentary lapse and forgets which end of the word (left or right) he's supposed to use as his starting point.

Capital letters in the wrong places

The confusion surrounding letters like 'b' and 'd' may cause a dyslexic child to switch to capital letters when writing these letters (even in the middle of a word). Indeed, work that contains a strange mixture of lower-case and capital letters is another tell-tale sign of dyslexia, which may persist into his teenage years and beyond.

A dyslexic child might simply forget the difference between capital letters and small letters, because he never quite learned which is which. Many dyslexics also find it so hard to form letters on the page that they just stop using small letters altogether. As a coping strategy, therefore, a child may write in all capitals. Capital letters are usually easier to form, and there's no need to differentiate between upper-case and lower-case in the writing.

Not hearing the words correctly

Some dyslexics are also put at a disadvantage by not hearing words correctly. A child's spelling can be affected by a listening issue called auditory discrimination. He may struggle to hear the difference between similar sounds, such as /f/ (*fuh*, as in 'find') and /θ/ (*thuh*, as in 'think'). Little wonder he misspells 'with' as *wif*, then!

These auditory issues may also make it harder for him to follow where the spaces between words lie. He may hear 'celebrate' as two or three words, and therefore spell it as *sell or rent*. 'Respite' may be heard as *rest bite*, and spelled accordingly. (Read more about auditory discrimination in *Chapter 8: Speaking and Listening*.)

Spelling in the classroom

The way that schools teach spelling makes things even harder for dyslexic children. In class, a teacher may recite the letters of a spelling for a child to write down. For example: 'A-P-P-L-E, apple'. This poses a number of problems for a dyslexic child.

Poor auditory discrimination means he may not even hear the sounds correctly. He'll also have trouble with sequencing. So, even if he hears correctly, he'll struggle to write down the letters in the right order.

Plus, a dyslexic child's weak working memory is taxed when he has to do several things at once. In this case, he must listen to a letter-sound spoken aloud (/eɪ/ or *ay*, as in 'lane'), then code it into a phonetic sound (/æ/ or *ah*, as in 'hat'), and then form a letter on the page (a). The result: memory overload!

Another classic teacher technique is to give a child a dictionary. If a child spells a word incorrectly, the teacher tells him to look up the correct spelling in the dictionary. However, a dyslexic child's visual memory of the word is likely to be fuzzy. He may not have even a rough idea of how it's spelled. This means he can't even begin to find the right page in the dictionary. Even if he can work out the first few letters, he might not have mastered his alphabet well enough to navigate the dictionary. (Most dyslexics continue to sing the alphabet from the beginning each time they want to locate a letter's position.)

Unable to visualise spellings

Many traditional teaching methods clash with the way dyslexics learn. When teaching the class to spell, a teacher will often expect children to picture the word in their mind's eye. It's this 'visualising' that makes it easier for non-dyslexic children to transfer a spelling from their minds on to a sheet of paper.

However, visualising spellings is difficult for many dyslexic children. Weak working memory makes holding a spelling in your mind really hard. And, if he can't 'see' a word in his mind, it becomes much harder for him to write it down – especially if it's a long word.

Due to weak working memory or visual distortion, many dyslexic children have trouble accurately copying spellings from the board or worksheet. Even though the word is right in front of him, he may not be able to hold it in his working memory and write it down correctly. Incorrect spellings of days of the week and months of the year (despite the child writing them over and over again for years) can be a dyslexia red flag.

Putting spellings into practice

The dyslexia traits that make spelling harder (like weak working memory and left/right confusion) tend to get worse when a child is under pressure or multi-tasking.

Many dyslexics, like Anthony (see case study), simply never get the hang of spelling at all. Many more, like Maisie (see case study), work overtime to get all of their spellings correct in spelling tests. Yet these spellings may go downhill when they're writing in class. Once he has to concentrate on ordering his thoughts and answering the question, writing neatly and using punctuation, his working memory is too overloaded to also process the correct spellings. Unlike Maisie's teacher, however, we can see that this isn't sloppiness – it's dyslexia, and it can be supported.

EXAMPLES OF DYSLEXIC SPELLING

The way a dyslexic child spells will look different depending on his age. Here are some broad examples of what dyslexic spelling might look like in younger and older children:

> **Six-year-old with dyslexia:**
>
> miy techr seb i LuT neb To Lurn mi k wbs
> *(My teacher said I need to learn my key words.)*
>
> **Eight-year-old with dyslexia:**
>
> my teecher siad I need triy harDer at speling and not Be laizey
> *(My teacher said I need to try harder at spelling and not be lazy.)*
>
> **Ten-year-old with dyslexia:**
>
> My werk comes back whith, halve off everyfink crossed out nowe I jut aviod words I ca'nt spell
> *(My work comes back with half of everything crossed out. Now I just avoid words I can't spell.)*
>
> **Fourteen-year-old with dyslexia:**
>
> My teachers Bang on about the the importense of spelling sow I just pritenD check my work I Don't see the point.

(My teachers bang on about the importance of spelling, so I just pretend to check my work. I don't see the point.)

SPELLING – KEY SIGNS OF DYSLEXIA:

- Child continues to use phonetic spellings, even as he gets older
- Confused by homophones
- Spells the same word two or more different ways on a single page
- Jumbles up letters within a word
- Forms letters back-to-front
- Uses a strange mix of small letters and capitals
- Unable/unwilling to use a dictionary
- Copies words from the board incorrectly
- Spells much better during a spelling test than in written work

Case study: Anthony, who couldn't even spell his own name (part 1)

Even though he was eight years old, Anthony sometimes spelled his own name wrong! He wrote 'Antoyne' instead of 'Anthony'.

When Anthony brought home lists of spelling words to learn, his mum clucked at him. 'Anthony,' she said, 'you haven't even copied these down correctly!'

His mum thought he was just scatter-brained, but Anthony's school thought he was stupid. They put him on the 'red' table – and everyone knew that the red table was really the slow table. Anthony didn't like being on the slow table, but he supposed it was true. He *was* slow. It took him ages to write anything, because he found spelling so hard.

Yet Anthony was *bored* on the red table. His mind was always racing; his imagination spilling over. If anyone asked Anthony to tell a story, he'd light up. He was great at coming up with stories: ones about ghosts and monsters and great big scary bears! But when he tried to write down his stories (*gosts and monstas and grat big scare bars*), his work came back covered in corrections from the teacher.

Case study: Maisie and the Isle of Wight (part 1)

'I know you can spell these words. You're just being sloppy!' the teacher told Maisie.

Maisie turned red. It was true that she always got 10 out of 10 on her spelling tests. But, when she tried to write in class, she ended up spelling those same words wrong. Her teacher was always going *tut-tut-tut* and saying her work was sloppy. But Maisie wasn't sloppy! She tried really hard!

'Why are you spelling *white* like this?' the teacher asked. 'You're a clever girl, but you're just being careless!'

Maisie looked at the word which was circled in green pen. *Wight*. Wasn't that how you spelled the colour? Maisie was sure it was, because her nan had sent her a postcard from the Isle of Wight (she kept it pinned next to her bed) and that was how the postcard spelled it.

Maisie slunk back to her seat, feeling confused and ashamed.

SUPPORTING DYSLEXIA

Play to your child's strengths

Whether your child's problems with spelling are obvious (like Anthony's) or hidden beneath the surface (like Maisie's), spelling doesn't have to remain an Achilles' heel. Dyslexic spellers just have to use different techniques – ones that play to their strengths.

Joined-up handwriting

Surprising as it may seem, in my experience, the best way to improve a dyslexic child's spelling is to improve his handwriting. This is because when you write using fully joined-up handwriting (called continuous cursive) you build up muscle memory.

It may be boring, but if a child writes a word twenty times using continuous cursive, the muscles of his hand will start to retain the spelling. It's the process of joining, where every letter connects to the next one, that keeps a dyslexic anchored in the right spelling. This means he doesn't have to rely on 'visualising' a spelling using his working memory. Instead, the muscles of his hand will remember the spelling for him.

Ironically, if a child struggles with reading and writing, some teachers will discourage him from learning joined-up handwriting. This is a classic mistake. Dyslexia isn't stupidity and, assuming he's not struggling physically (see *Chapter 10: Movement*), joined-up handwriting isn't 'too hard' for him to master. In fact, it could make all the difference.

Letting a dyslexic child slip into using un-joined-up handwriting or all-capitals is a recipe for disaster. It's true that he may hate joined-up handwriting at first, for a few different reasons. He may find the physical act of writing hard. Or he may never have fully learned to join his handwriting in the first place. However, it's worth persevering, because I have found that spelling-via-muscle-memory works best if you write in fully joined-up handwriting.

True continuous cursive includes joining each 'y' (by looping it) and dotting 'i' only at the end of the word. Some British schools have handwriting policies which suggest that certain letters (such as 'y') should not be joined. For a dyslexic child, however, joining *all* the letters is important. It may be worth sharing this book with your child's teacher, so that they understand why you are encouraging your child to use true continuous cursive.

Touch-typing

Learning to touch-type can have the same effect as joined-up handwriting. There are plenty of free online courses for touch-typing, using the little nubs on the F and J keys to guide the hands. Touch-typing, like writing in cursive, means that his working memory doesn't have to do all the work. It's the fingers that automatically remember how to spell a word correctly.

Most children will probably prefer to learn to touch-type, rather than learn joined-up handwriting. But it's worth trying out both. After all, he won't always have access to a computer keyboard, but he will always have his hands. (Hopefully. As long as he doesn't become a pirate!)

A word of caution: if an older child has been spelling a word incorrectly for a long time, he will already have built up muscle memory for the wrong spelling. This means he will have to create a new (correct) muscle memory. It's perfectly possible to do this – it just requires repetition. The child will just need to write out in cursive (or touch-type) the correct spelling even more times, to override the old muscle memory.

Talking it through

Helping a dyslexic speller also requires taking a new perspective. In schools, children are usually expected to simply 'absorb' spelling rules. However, dyslexics find it much easier to learn if these rules are explained to them.

Therefore, it's important to draw attention to the special features of a spelling. For example, 'replayed' has 're' as its prefix (beginning), 'ed' as its suffix (ending), and 'ay' is its vowel sound.

When talking it through, also try to explain the story behind a word. When your child gets stuck on a word, don't just say 'it's spelled that way because it is'. Find a better answer for him, by delving into the basics of etymology (the study of the history of words). Etymology can engage a child and help him to remember how to read a word.

After all, it's much easier to master a strange word if someone tells you why it's strange. For example, 'knight' is spelled with a K, because in the language of Old English, spoken during the Middle Ages, everyone said the /k/ sound aloud. This fun fact transforms a nonsense rule into something that's alive with meaning.

Tools and tricks for remembering

A dyslexic child can benefit from using props when learning to spell. It may help him to have the letters of the alphabet spread out in front of him, to look at and touch. This means there's no need to visualise letters – he can reach out and grab them! Make your own tactile letters (from sandpaper, fabric or wood), or buy a set of letters.

Magnetic letters, perhaps in a cursive font, can particularly help children who have trouble forming their letters correctly. Asking a child to spell using the magnetic letters can be a bridge that leads him into writing spellings correctly.

Dyslexics may also need a 'crutch' to help them to remember certain difficult words. Mnemonics (memory aids) can be useful. Try replacing each letter of a tricky spelling with a word, creating a funny (and visually stimulating) sentence.

Take 'because', for example. B-E-C-A-U-S-E becomes 'Big Elephants Can Add Up Sums Easily'. The child can picture a clever elephant doing maths. (The ones normally taught in schools – 'Big Elephants Can Always Understand Small Elephants' or 'Big Elephants Can't Always Use Small Exits' are more visually pleasing, but they rely on a child who struggles with spelling knowing that the word 'always' starts with an 'a', rather than an 'o', as many dyslexics will assume ['orlways'].) Armed with a mnemonic, spelling 'because' no longer triggers a panicked blank. The child just has to think about elephants and remember the mnemonic.

(Ironically, most dyslexics could use a mnemonic to remember how to spell 'mnemonic'!)

Splitting spellings into chunks

A long word also becomes easier to remember if it's broken down into smaller chunks. Take the word 'separated', for example, which is one of the most commonly misspelled words in the English language. Splitting 'separated' into chunks produces: **sep / a rat / ed**.

The first chunk, 'sep', is easy to remember, because it's spelled the way it sounds. The last chunk, 'ed', is a very common word ending. Plus, there's the memorable image of 'a rat' in the middle of the word. Chunking long words in this way is helpful, because it reduces the pressure on the child's working memory.

Don't be afraid to add movement and an element of play to the process of learning spellings, either. Adding an action or singing makes 'chunks' more likely to lodge in a dyslexic child's memory.

Playing patty cake, where you chant each letter of a spelling when you slap hands, triggers a 'learning by doing' instinct and gives physical feedback. Making a spelling into a song or rap (there are some great apps for this) can also turn boring spelling practice into something fun and memorable.

Beware spell checkers!

But wait a minute. Who needs to learn to spell when you have a computer spell checker?

Unfortunately, traditional computer spell checkers won't correct common dyslexic errors, because many of these errors involve phonetic spelling. Take the example of 'because' again, which a dyslexic might spell phonetically: 'bicuz'. Microsoft Word's spell checker will replace that spelling with 'bikes', not 'because'!

That said, there are now alternative computer spell checkers available, designed with dyslexics in mind. These spell checkers, examples of which include *Ginger*, *Ghotit*, and *Verity Spell*, recognise phonetic spellings and they give spelling suggestions based on the context of the sentence.

There are low-tech spelling aids available, too. A phonetic dictionary, such as the ACE Spelling Dictionary, is just like a regular dictionary, but it allows you to look up words based on how they sound. So, 'pneumonia' wouldn't just be listed under P. It would also be listed under N and OO. Handy!

Although spelling can be tough for a dyslexic child, in the long run he may turn out to be a better-than-average speller, as a result of regular practice and a deep understanding of the English language. His peers may get tripped up by new words, but a dyslexic child who has learned the spelling rules inside-out can take on a big word with no problem!

SPELLING – KEY SUPPORT FOR DYSLEXIA:

- Encourage joined-up handwriting or touch-typing
- Use tactile or magnetic letters to form words
- Use phonetic dictionaries and clever computer spell checkers
- Come up with mnemonics and tricks for remembering
- Break down spellings into chunks
- Use music and action during spelling
- Point out the special features of every spelling
- Highlight links between words that follow the same spelling rules
- Recap and 'overlearn' the most commonly used words, so that they become automatic

Case study: Anthony, who couldn't even spell his own name (part 2)

When Anthony's mum made him start writing in joined-up handwriting, he didn't really like it. In fact, he hated it! He couldn't see that it made *any* difference to his spelling. He only did it because it earned him stars on his reward chart.

A few weeks later, Anthony found his mum looking over some of his schoolwork. Each sheet of work had his name and the date written in cursive at the top of the page.

'Notice anything?' his mum asked.

'No,' Anthony said.

'You've spelled your name right on every single one of these,' she said.

Anthony was too cool to tell his mum just how happy that made him, but he started to take pride in his newfound abilities.

Case study: Maisie and the Isle of Wight (part 2)

Maisie did so well on her spelling tests that her teacher assumed she couldn't be dyslexic. What the teacher didn't know was that Maisie had forgotten most of her spelling words by the day after the spelling test.

However, when Maisie's dad started to work with her

at home, she actually began to understand spelling rules. The two of them played lots of spelling games and talked about how spellings were put together. Slowly but surely, Maisie's spelling in her written work began to improve.

Maisie still has her nan's postcard pinned up in her bedroom, but now she knows that the colour is spelled *white*, not *Wight*.

7.

WRITING

> '6 9
>
> 'I write children's books – and I'm in the bottom
> three percent of people academically in America.'
> — HENRY WINKLER (dyslexic author and actor)
> Star of Happy Days and best-selling author

IT'S NOT JUST POOR SPELLING AND BACK-TO-FRONT LETTERS THAT may make a dyslexic child's written work hard to read. Dyslexic problems with ordering her thoughts may mean that the child's writing is rambling, incomplete, and a poor reflection of her true intelligence.

SIGNS OF DYSLEXIA

The gap between reading and writing ability

We tend to think that reading and writing go hand-in-hand. If a child can read, we assume it will be easy for her to learn to write, as well. In fact, for most dyslexic children, this is not the case.

Many parents find that their child shows a big gap between her 'reading age' and her 'writing age'. This gap may be as large as three or four years, so a child might have a reading age of 12, but she'll only be writing on the same level as an eight-year-old.

A high reading age and a low writing age are especially common if the child is a 'muddler'. She might be able to muddle through reading by memorising some words and guessing at the rest. But, when she has to write, these strategies don't work.

Process vs. thoughts

As we write, we have to concentrate on two things: what we're going to write (our thoughts), and how we're going to write it (the process of writing, including spelling, structure, and handwriting). The more comfortable we are with the process of writing, the more energy we can devote to our thoughts.

It's been estimated that, when writing:

- Non-dyslexic children spend 90% of their energy on thought and 10% on the process of writing.
- Dyslexic children spend 90% of their energy on the process of writing and 10% on thought.

Why is this? Well, a big part of it can be traced back to weak working memory, which is a key dyslexia trait.

This memory issue means that a dyslexic child can only hold a few items in her mind at once. Yet writing is a complex process, which involves juggling many different skills. For a typical written assignment, we have to:

1. Come up with ideas
2. Put our thoughts in order
3. Answer the question
4. Remember how to form letters correctly
5. Remember spelling, punctuation, and grammar rules
6. Choose words carefully to make it interesting to read

That's a lot of multi-tasking!

For a typical dyslexic child with a weak working memory, it will be a problem. She'll work more slowly than her classmates and struggle to get everything right first time.

Problems with reading the question

What's more, if a child is a 'muddler', she might only have a shaky grasp of phonics patterns (the sounds that make up words) and how to read words on the page.

This means that just reading the question for an exam or homework assignment can pose a problem. Most dyslexic children will do one of the following:

1.   Not read the question properly

Because she finds reading hard work, a dyslexic child may skim or 'half-read' the question. As a result, she won't fully understand what she's been asked to write. Her written work may fail to answer the question.

2.   Read and re-read the question

Alternatively, a dyslexic child may take so long to read the question that, by the time she gets to the end, she's forgotten the beginning. She has no choice but to go back to the beginning and read it again. She may end up learning it by heart. It will take her so long to read the question that she'll end up rushing through her written answer.

Good ideas, bad writing

Even if a dyslexic child manages to read the question properly without wasting too much time, she may have trouble getting her thoughts down on to paper. No matter how good her imagination, a dyslexic child is likely to devolve into writing drivel if she's not supported properly.

As I discussed in *Chapter 5*, a non-dyslexic child may be able to hold a lot of different information in her working memory and manipulate that information easily. This means, if she's asked to write a story, she can juggle all of her story ideas and quickly put them down on paper in a sensible order.

However, a dyslexic child may struggle to hold even one story idea in her (weak) working memory. The rest of her ideas will drift away, out of her head, as she concentrates on writing down her first idea. The kicker is: since she can't remember the rest of her ideas, she may just write down her first idea over and over again.

Disordered thoughts and mad tangents

Even if a dyslexic child manages to get several ideas down on paper, she may not order her thoughts properly. The result may be a mish-mash of ideas, with no real structure. This is because sequencing (putting things in the right order) doesn't come naturally to most dyslexic children.

What's more, the dyslexic brain 'files' information in unusual ways. Dyslexic minds make unconventional connections. This can lead to amazing ideas and ingenious solutions to problems. (Find out more in *Chapter 14: Problem Solving*.) But, when she's writing, it may cause her to go off on a mad tangent. When she's asked to write about the life cycle of a tadpole, for example, a dyslexic child may end up writing about her holiday to France, because she ate frog's legs while she was there!

Ordinarily, a child might combat disordered thoughts by checking her work and rewriting. Unfortunately, a dyslexic child may be particularly reluctant to check her work after she has finished writing. In contrast to a child of low intellect, a dyslexic child will *know* that she has made mistakes in her writing – and she'll care deeply. She won't want to check her work and see the mistakes, knowing that perhaps she doesn't have the skills or energy to fix those mistakes. It's too demoralising. She'll either refuse outright, or simply *pretend* to check over her work.

Untidy handwriting

Parents may also find that a dyslexic child's work is particularly hard to check – due to her handwriting! Surprising as it may seem, scruffy handwriting can be another tell-tale sign of dyslexia.

There are two reasons a dyslexic child's handwriting might be untidy:

1. *Defence mechanism*

If a child's writing is so untidy that it's almost impossible to read, then it stands to reason people won't read it. Teachers won't be able to mark the work and a dyslexic child's problems with writing won't be found out.

2. *It hurts to write*

Due to underlying problems with dyspraxia, a child might struggle to grip her pen correctly and control the muscles in her hand.

Gripping a pen may seem straightforward, but it actually requires lots of small muscles in our hands to work together. This is called fine motor control and it can prove particularly difficult for a dyslexic child with dyspraxia symptoms. She might press too hard on the paper. She might bend her thumb backwards in an awkward grip, or cross her thumb over the pen to lock her hand into place. All of this makes writing literally hurt. Little wonder she doesn't enjoy it! (Find out more about dyspraxia in *Chapter 10: Movement*.)

Dyslexic problems with writing are wide-ranging, and there can be knock-on effects for all of a child's school subjects. (After all, even scientists need to explain their theories!) Some children, like Liam (see case study), find that it negatively affects family life. It's true that dyslexia traits may make writing harder (and slower) for some children, but, with the right support, any dyslexic child can become a confident writer.

Writing – Key Signs of Dyslexia:

- Child is bright and curious in person, but her writing is of poor quality
- Big gap between reading and writing ability
- Only pretends to check through work
- Responses don't answer the question
- Writing is structured poorly
- Writing contains tangents and non sequiturs
- Scruffy handwriting (especially when spelling a tricky word)

Case study: Liam, who hated weekends (part 1)

Other children spent their weekends doing karate or going swimming. Not Liam.

Sometimes his family planned to do fun things at the weekend, but they never quite got around to it. Homework came first. And, for Liam, homework took *hours*.

At school, Liam's teachers were confused by his work. The homework he handed in was always excellent. However, when he sat exams, Liam did terribly. Since Liam's teachers knew he was very bright, when he worked slowly, they labelled him lazy, sloppy, and easily distracted. His perfect homework proved that he could work quickly and accurately at home.

What they didn't realise was that to write just three good sentences might take Liam half an hour, with his mum standing over him, helping. And a full homework assignment might take him the whole weekend.

Case study: Charlotte, who hated stories (part 1)

All of Charlotte's friends loved stories. They loved them so much that they stayed inside at school break-times to write stories of their own. But not Charlotte. Charlotte said she hated stories, so she went outside and played on her own.

Charlotte's parents were surprised when she was diagnosed with dyslexia. 'But she does so brilliantly at school!' they said. In fact, Charlotte's naturally strong long-term memory meant that she'd developed loads of strategies to deal with her hidden dyslexia.

It was in writing where her strong memory finally let her down. She found it so hard to start writing that every assignment was a rush job, and she hated to read through her work afterwards.

Writing was a *chore*. She thought her friends who loved to write were bonkers.

SUPPORTING DYSLEXIA

Getting ideas down on paper

Given a little thinking time, dyslexic children are not usually short of great ideas. Writing is frustrating precisely because they can't get their ideas down on paper. A new approach is needed for a dyslexic child – one that doesn't force her to rely on her (weak) working memory.

This is where brainstorming and diagrams can be useful: spider diagrams; star diagrams; Venn diagrams; fishbone diagrams; visual planners. Diagrams allow a dyslexic child to get her ideas down on paper in a fun, low-stress way. She doesn't have to worry about remembering her ideas when she starts to write. She can simply look at the diagram and see her next idea.

Paragraph organisers, a type of mnemonic (memory aid) that reminds your child what to include in her written work, can also be valuable. One example of a paragraph organiser is: P (point), E (explanation), E (example), L (link to next paragraph). This can help to give a structure and a starting point for writing.

Doing one thing at a time

When she has to write something, parents should help their child to focus on completing the work in stages. Breaking down the act of writing into chunks is a massive relief for a dyslexic child.

At school, when she is asked to write, her work is marked for content, spelling, vocabulary, proper capital letters, paragraphs, and much more. A dyslexic is likely to wilt under the pressure of getting everything right first time. However, by focusing on doing one thing at a time, the child is not overloading her working memory by doing too many things at once.

Writing in stages might look like this:

1. **Planning:** Write down ideas using a diagram or paragraph organiser.
2. **Planning:** Put ideas in the best order.
3. **Writing:** Expand ideas into full sentences.
4. **Checking:** Put capital letters in the right places.
5. **Checking:** Check the work makes sense, with no words missing.
6. **Checking:** Find and fix any spelling mistakes.
7. **Improving:** Add in or change words.

The list will get longer, depending on the child's age and ability, but the principle stays the same. Just concentrate on one part of writing, and then move on to the next part.

Redrafting and proofreading

This process of doing one thing at a time should help your child to begin to see any piece of writing as a work in progress. It's not something you just do and then leave. It's something that needs correcting and redrafting. Most dyslexics have a mental block when it comes to checking their work, so this is an area that needs to be worked on specifically.

Proofreading can be a touchy subject for any child. After all, she's spent ages on her work and she doesn't want it to be criticised. For this reason, asking a dyslexic child to check *someone else's* work is less emotional. In this way, the child gets used to the act of checking. Plus, she gets to feel smug, spotting someone else's mistakes and correcting their work. After a while, checking her *own* work will feel less scary.

Parents can create their own proofreading challenges for their child. Write a paragraph or just a sentence, putting in deliberate spelling mistakes, intentionally missing out letters, and omitting some punctuation and capital letters (e.g. 'i lik riddin miy bike' for *I like riding my bike*). You could even make it a routine: every morning, over breakfast, ask your child to correct a simple, error-filled sentence.

Writing for a reason

It's important to remember that, if the only time a child writes is when she has to complete a boring piece of homework, it stands to reason she won't enjoy it. For a dyslexic child, this fact is magnified.

Instead of just writing for the sake of writing, encourage your child to write for a reason. Get her writing postcards and letters to send. Find competitions to enter. Ask her to write stories, plays, blogs, diaries, emails, tweets. Even though writing may be more difficult for a dyslexic child, once she is able to start getting her ideas down on paper, there's often no stopping her. After all, some of our best storytellers are dyslexic ...

Mystery writer Agatha Christie is the best-selling novelist of all time. It's amazing to learn, then, that she struggled with writing and spelling her whole life. As a child, she was even considered the 'slow' one in her family! Experts now believe that she was probably dyslexic.

Other successful dyslexic storytellers include Lynda La Plante, creator of *Prime Suspect*, and John Irving, who won an Oscar for his screenplay, *The Cider House Rules*. Irving says that the process of overcoming his dyslexic difficulties made him hard-working and willing to push himself – exactly the qualities that make a great writer.

> ## WRITING – KEY SUPPORT FOR DYSLEXIA:
> - Create fun brainstorms before starting to write
> - Take writing one step at a time
> - Let your child check other people's work for mistakes
> - Write for fun – postcards, letters, stories, and more!

Case study: Liam, who hated weekends (part 2)

Liam's parents helped Liam to begin planning out his writing before he started. When he did one thing at a time, suddenly writing wasn't so overwhelming. Homework was still hard work for Liam, but it took so much less time!

Now Liam goes swimming at weekends, because all of his homework is finished by Saturday lunchtime. Things at school are better for Liam, too. Because the homework he hands in is now similar to his classwork, he is getting help at school to show his brilliant ideas.

Case study: Charlotte, who hated stories (part 2)

Once she began using spider diagrams to put her ideas down on paper, Charlotte stopped hating writing. In fact, she started to really *like* writing! Charlotte enjoyed writing stories so much that she entered a short story contest – and she won!

Now she spends break-times with her friends, writing about dragons and princesses and pirates.

8.

SPEAKING AND LISTENING

> 'Dyslexia doesn't mean that you're stupid. It just means that you work in a different way.'
> — **KEIRA KNIGHTLEY (dyslexic actor)**
> *Oscar-nominated star of* Pride and Prejudice *and* Pirates of the Caribbean

MOST PARENTS WON'T CONNECT THEIR CHILD'S VERBAL slip-ups with dyslexia, even though it might be the root cause. Many dyslexics have problems hearing similar sounds, and the unconventional connections made by their highly creative minds can affect how they speak, too.

SIGNS OF DYSLEXIA

When speaking is easy ... and when it isn't

Not all dyslexic children have problems with their speech. In fact, many children have better-than-average verbal abilities. For a dyslexic child who's keen to express himself, talking is often much easier than writing!

This type of dyslexic child might become a great performer, as he takes every opportunity to practise speaking. His only problem is that being very articulate may mask his dyslexic difficulties with reading and writing.

By contrast, a different dyslexic child may have underlying problems with speaking and listening. He may be more likely to make verbal slip-ups, like saying 'massif' instead of 'massive'. The problem is: this child doesn't hear what other people hear; a condition called poor auditory discrimination.

Auditory discrimination

Auditory discrimination has nothing to do with the ears. It's all about how the brain processes what we hear. If a child has poor auditory discrimination abilities, he can't process the difference between similar sounds.

Saying 'anyfing' instead of 'anything' may seem like it has nuffing (sorry, *nothing*) to do with dyslexia. But it actually has everyfing (sorry, *everything*) to do with dyslexia! Poor auditory discrimination doesn't *just* affect dyslexic children, but dyslexic children are more likely to have problems with auditory discrimination.

The sounds /f/ (*fuh*, as in 'find'), /θ/ (*thuh*, as in 'think') and /v/ (*vuh*, as in 'van') are three of the most similar in the English language. The brain has to work incredibly hard to tell the difference between these sounds. And, if a child has poor skills in auditory discrimination, he's more likely to mix them up. This means a child can't hear the difference between 'nothing' and 'nuffing' or 'massive' and 'massif'. So it's very likely that he'll end up saying the word wrong, too.

'He's not dyslexic, he's just a Londoner!' I hear you cry. It's true that some regional accents are filled with alternative pronunciations. And it can be a matter of local pride to replace /θ/ (*thuh*) with /f/ (*fuh*) in a word.

What's important to find out is whether your child is making these kinds of alterations on purpose. If he's saying 'anyfing' to fit in with his friends, that's not dyslexia. But if he's saying 'anyfing' because he literally can't hear the difference, then that's poor auditory discrimination – and a possible sign of dyslexia.

Similar sounds

Mix-ups involving /θ/ (*thuh*), /f/ (*fuh*) and /v/ (*vuh*) may be among the most common errors, but the English language is filled with very similar sounds. The difference between how we say words like 'put' and 'but', 'peg' and 'pig' is absolutely tiny. It's especially hard to process the medial (middle) sounds in a word.

The following are similar speech sounds that can cause particular problems:

/f/ (fuh) ←→ /θ/ (thuh) ←→ /v/ (vuh)

fing (thing), massif (massive)

/m/ (muh) ←→ /n/ (nuh)

imput (input), discrinimation (discrimination)

/w/ (wuh) ←→ /r/ (ruh)

wunning (running)

/tʃ/ (chuh) ←→ /ʃ/ (shh)

choe (shoe)

/e/ (eh) ←→ /ɪ/ (ih)

peg (pig)

/p/ (puh) ←→ /b/ (buh)

put (but)

Clues in spelling

Poor auditory discrimination doesn't just affect speech – it affects spelling, too. It stands to reason that if a child can't hear the difference between certain sounds, he'll probably spell words wrongly, too.

Be on the lookout in your child's written work for spellings that mix up similar speech sounds over and over again. If he keeps spelling a word wrongly, it may mean that he isn't properly hearing the way it's pronounced. This can be particularly noticeable when he has to spell a rare word that he may never have seen written down. So he has to rely completely on what he hears (e.g. writing 'watercall' instead of 'waterfall').

Mixed-up words

It's not just auditory discrimination that can make speaking a problem for dyslexics. A dyslexic child may also find it hard to put sounds in the right order (sequencing). This can lead to verbal mix-ups. He may say the syllables within a word out of order, or the words within a sentence out of order. Examples:

> **Animal → Aminal**
> **Bubble bath → Bath bubble**
> **Ice-cream cone → Ice-cone cream**

A dyslexic child may also make Spoonerisms. This means he'll accidentally mix up the first letters of each word in a phrase. Examples:

> **Field of sheep → Shield of feep**
> **Lawn mower → Mawn lower**

All children make these types of mistakes as they learn to speak. The difference with dyslexic children is that they don't simply grow out of it.

Disordered thoughts = disordered speech

Poor auditory discrimination and problems with sequencing may have the biggest effect on how a dyslexic child pronounces words. However, other dyslexia traits can also affect his speech in conversation or when he needs to explain something. In fact, parents may see the problems their dyslexic child has with writing repeated in his speech. A dyslexic child may find it hard to order his thoughts when he's speaking, just the same as when he's writing.

Ask a dyslexic child a question about how much rain there is in the rainforest and, instead of answering the question, he may just tell you everything he knows about the rainforest. His weak working memory makes it hard work to retrieve the correct information, process it, and then shape it into a short answer. What he gets instead is a 'memory overload!' signal. In desperation, he'll just spill out everything he knows on the topic, like verbal diarrhoea.

He may even go off on tangents as he answers the question. His brain is making unconventional connections as he retrieves information from his memory. So what seems like a clear association to him may seem like a crazy tangent to the listener. (Find out more about how dyslexic minds retrieve information in *Chapter 14: Problem Solving*.)

In the classroom, weak working memory may also mean that a dyslexic child can't keep a thought in his head without voicing it. Instead of raising his hand and waiting until he's called upon in class, he may shout out the answer. During a conversation, he may interrupt constantly.

This isn't because of poor impulse control, or because he doesn't understand the social 'rules' of the situation. It's simply because he has something to say and he knows he'll forget it if he doesn't say it *right now*.

Thingamy and whatsit

Another dyslexic weakness lies in 'rapid naming' (also called 'word-finding difficulties'). This is the idea that when someone shows you a picture of a post box, the word just pops into your head and you say, 'It's a post box!' For a dyslexic, however, the word *doesn't* just pop into his head. He might say, 'It's that big red thing you put letters in'. Or he'll simply call it 'thingamy'. He may even say the wrong word completely and call it a lamp post or a parking meter.

We all have blank moments when we can't remember the name of something, so we just say, 'Oh, you know, whatsit.' However, for dyslexics, these aren't rare moments. This is another case of the dyslexic brain's 'unconventional filing system' in action. Retrieving information isn't a straightforward process – and it can take time. This child isn't stupid; he knows what a post box is. It just takes longer than average for him to name an object, and there's a chance he might name it wrongly.

Severe speech impediments

For most dyslexic children, their speech problems will be mild. However, if a child also has dyspraxia symptoms, he may find it hard to coordinate the muscles in his face, mouth, and tongue.

'Verbal dyspraxia' or 'oral motor dyspraxia' may mean that the child cannot speak clearly. The condition makes it hard for his body and his brain to communicate properly. He may have trouble getting the right muscles in his mouth to work, in order to say what he wants to say. (Find out more about dyspraxia in *Chapter 10: Movement*.)

Verbal dyspraxia, in combination with poor auditory discrimination, may produce a severe speech impediment. Further speech problems (such as delayed speech) can also result from dyslexia co-occurring with Autism Spectrum

Disorder. (Find out more about Autism Spectrum Disorder in *Chapter 15: Co-occurring Conditions.*)

Range of abilities

When it comes to speaking and listening, it's common to see a range of different abilities in dyslexic children. One dyslexic child might be reluctant to speak, for fear of revealing his speech impediment. Another, like Alexander (see case study), might be the loudest, chattiest, most articulate child in the room.

Neither child needs to be resigned to a particular fate. The loud, chatty child can become a bookworm with the right support. And the child with the speech impediment can begin to re-train his ear. By building up good strategies for speaking and listening, any dyslexic child can become the chattiest one in the room – if he so chooses.

SPEAKING AND LISTENING – KEY SIGNS OF DYSLEXIA:

- Child mispronounces similar speech sounds
- Uses Spoonerisms and mixed-up words
- Calls objects 'thingamy' or uses the wrong word completely
- Slips into verbal diarrhoea when asked a question
- Shouts out answers in class

Case study: Lola and the elephants (part 1)

When Lola had to give a presentation on the Ancient Egyptians in front of her whole class, she wasn't worried. She loved the Egyptians – with their funny hieroglyphics and enormous pyramids – and she was sure she could find loads of things to say.

But, when Lola stepped up in front of the blackboard to give her presentation, she froze.

Long seconds passed. When Lola still didn't say anything, her teacher prompted her: 'Why don't you tell us why the Ancient Egyptians built the pyramids, Lola?'

Lola took a deep breath and began to speak. 'The pyramids were massif. They were really huge ...'

Lola talked and talked and talked. She told the class everything she could remember about the pyramids. And, when she couldn't remember anything else about them, she just kept talking.

'Okay, Lola,' her teacher said, interrupting her. 'I don't think we need to hear anything else about your trip to the zoo.'

'But ... but,' Lola said desperately, 'I saw an ephelant there, and there were ephelants in Ancient Egypt, too!'

A couple of people laughed and Lola felt her face burn.

Case study: Alexander the Great (part 1)

Alexander could talk to anyone. He didn't just talk to children his own age, but also to friends of his parents, train conductors, museum staff, the little old ladies who served cups of tea in the café ...

Everyone agreed that Alexander was so bright, so clever and *so* articulate. His ambition was to be a presenter on one of those really serious historical TV programmes.

At the weekends and during the school holidays, Alexander's parents took him on trips to museums, stately homes, historical sites, and – best of all – castles!

Alexander loved to stride around castles and talk to people and soak in the history of the place.

Yet his parents couldn't understand why Alexander didn't get better grades in school, especially in his beloved subject of history. Was he bored? Was the work too easy? Why did Alexander – who, in person, was a budding Simon Schama – never do well in history exams?

SUPPORTING DYSLEXIA

Re-training the ear

It is estimated that 10% of children have difficulties in speech and language that require long-term support. So, if your child has problems with speaking, he certainly isn't alone!

Yet speech impediments don't need to be a permanent part of your child's life. It's perfectly possible to re-train the ear to hear sounds correctly and improve his speech. Even if a child can't hear the difference between similar sounds at first, he can develop that ability – and begin to speak confidently.

Speech therapy

A speech and language therapist can teach your child how to move his lips, mouth, and tongue to say words correctly. He or she can also help your child to improve auditory discrimination, rapid naming, and phonological awareness. Even children with mild speech problems can benefit from speech therapy. Don't be put off by the stigma of it. A few sessions may be all that it takes to get him on the right track.

You can also help your child at home, by teaching him how to shape his mouth when he says certain words. Sit side-by-side with your child and look in the mirror together. Both of you say a word that he has trouble pronouncing. Then compare how the two of you pronounce that word. Once your child can see and feel the difference between how he says a word and how you say a word, he'll begin to understand where he's going wrong.

Much of speech therapy is about exaggeration. In everyday speech, the way we pronounce sounds can look awfully alike. But, if we exaggerate how we say sounds, the differences become more distinct. Making funny faces as we exaggerate words also makes speech therapy more fun!

Practice makes perfect

If your child has trouble saying long words, slow down and break up the word into chunks. This makes it more likely to stick. In this way, 'animal' becomes 'an-im-al'. Use clapping or jumping to accompany each chunk, in order to make the process more fun and physical.

Practice makes perfect, so encourage your child to keep repeating a word with which he has trouble. Identify your child's most frequently mispronounced words and work on these first, perhaps framing it as the 'word of the week' or 'word of the month'. (Remember the **Rule of Ten**! A dyslexic child usually needs to practise a new skill ten times more than a non-dyslexic child.)

Of course, fixing speech problems can be a sensitive matter. Parents may find they're reluctant to criticise their child's speech. Many parents view their child's verbal slip-ups as a core part of him. 'That's just how he *is*,' they might say. Indeed, mixing up letters and words can be endearing.

However, it is important to point out and correct his mistakes. Making constant corrections may seem harsh, but he'll thank you for it in the long run. After all, a five-year-old who says 'aminal' is cute; a fifteen-year-old isn't.

There's no need to nag. Just make the correction – 'you mean animal, not aminal' – and move on. If your child makes a lot of speaking faults, don't try and work on everything at once. The child will be overwhelmed and feel like you're 'getting at him'. Instead, correct one speaking fault at a time.

Be (over)prepared

Fixing the 'verbal diarrhoea' aspect of dyslexia simply involves recognising the problem – and learning how to compensate for it. During oral exams or presentations, many children simply parrot information that they've memorised. Others decide to just 'wing it'. Dyslexic children, however, can't rely on memorisation or leaving things to chance.

Therefore, it's important for a dyslexic child to understand his topic on a deeper level. If he has to give a talk in school, he'll need to prepare in depth. Note cards might seem nerdy, but they'll keep him on track. And, because he really understands his subject (rather than just memorising facts), he can work around his dyslexic 'blank moments'.

The next great performer

With the right strategies in place, any dyslexic child can overcome his verbal slip-ups and learn to be more focused when he speaks. He might even be the next great performer. After all, if you take a look at the red carpet at the Oscars or the Grammys, you'll find a wealth of dyslexic stars.

Actors Whoopi Goldberg (*Sister Act*), Orlando Bloom (*Lord of the Rings*), Keira Knightley (*Pirates of the Caribbean*), and even The Fonz himself, Henry Winkler (*Happy Days*), are all dyslexic. They're joined by popstars Cher and Florence Welch (of Florence and the Machine), rockstar Noel Gallagher (of Oasis), and comedian Eddie Izzard. There are probably many more without diagnoses ...

A lot of dyslexic children actually develop better-than-average speaking skills. They find it hard to express themselves through writing, so they learn to make themselves heard!

SPEAKING AND LISTENING – KEY SUPPORT
FOR DYSLEXIA:

- Consider visiting a speech therapist or elocution teacher
- Try simple speech therapy exercises at home
- Break up difficult words into chunks
- Make gentle corrections when your child pronounces a word incorrectly
- Help him to over-prepare for public speaking

Case study: Lola and the elephants (part 2)

Lola's mum had noticed the slip-ups that Lola sometimes made when she talked, but she'd never thought anything of them. She certainly never thought Lola would get teased about them. But, when Lola came home in tears after her presentation, her mum decided it was time to do something.

Lola's mum arranged for Lola to visit a speech and language therapist. As a result, Lola's speech improved quickly. Nowadays, Lola makes far fewer slip-ups when she's talking. But, if she does make a silly mistake and someone teases her, she just laughs it off.

When Lola was due to give another presentation in school, her dad helped her to prepare note cards. 'It's the same thing I do when I have a big meeting at work,' he told her.

That made Lola feel very important. And, when she stood up in front of her class – to talk about the Tudors and Stuarts this time – she didn't freeze up or panic. When she finished her talk, the whole class clapped. Lola turned bright red – with pride.

Case study: Alexander the Great (part 2)

Alexander was so bright, so clever and *so* articulate that it never occurred to his parents that he could be dyslexic.

However, after he was diagnosed with dyslexia, Alexander's whole worldview changed. Secretly, he'd always felt like a faker. He loved history, but he couldn't read half of what was written on the signs at the museums he visited. His room was filled with big, fat history books – most of which he'd never read.

Alexander's parents took him for regular sessions with a personal tutor, who helped him to improve his reading and writing. Because Alexander really was so bright and so clever, he made quick progress, once things were explained to him in a way that he understood.

Now Alexander has begun to actually read those great big history books – and he's more in love with history than ever.

9.

MATHS

"

'I'm very open about my dyslexia. It's part of who I am and it's made me who I am. If you want strategic thinking, come to me. If you want linear thinking, don't come to me.'
— DIANE SWONK **(dyslexic economist)**
Chief economist for a top US financial services firm

THE SAME WEAKNESSES THAT MAKE IT HARDER FOR A DYSLEXIC child to learn to read can also make it harder for her to learn maths. In fact, for many children, maths is their weakest area, where dyslexia has the biggest impact on learning.

SIGNS OF DYSLEXIA

When hard is easy and easy is hard

In general, dyslexic children struggle with the 'nuts and bolts' of maths, such as times tables, but *not* the tricky part of understanding maths concepts. Ironically, this means they usually have the hard stuff figured out, but they fall down on the 'easy' stuff. A dyslexic child might understand the point of a maths problem (she gets *what* she's supposed to be finding out and *why*), but she simply can't get to the right answer.

This is because dyslexic children tend to have trouble grasping 'number facts'. Number facts are the absolute basics of maths, such as times tables, number bonds (e.g. two numbers that add up to 10), odds and evens, doubles and halves. Number facts make it much easier to do simple arithmetic. Without them, even 'easy' sums become hard.

This imbalance of skills (good non-verbal reasoning; bad grasp of number facts) can make a dyslexic child's progress in maths much slower that it should be. As a result, she might be near the bottom of her class, when she should be average or better. Or she could be in the middle of the pack, when she should be top of the class.

Using fingers and other crutches

Many dyslexic children will 'muddle through' maths, just as they do with reading. Instead of knowing her number bonds and times tables, a dyslexic child may rely on a crutch for her maths. She'll use her fingers to count – at an age when most of her classmates can do sums in their heads. Or she'll use pen and paper to work out even the simplest of sums, such as **6 – 4**.

Some children even come up with very clever (and, to outsiders, very *weird*) strategies to compensate for their weak grasp of number facts. A dyslexic child might go through a series of complicated steps to solve a sum like **7 x 2**, while her non-dyslexic classmate would 'just know' the answer, thanks to an understanding of doubling.

Not knowing if a number is big or small

A child who has serious dyslexic difficulties that affect her maths may have very poor 'number sense'. She can't get her head around the basic idea of what a number looks like in real terms. We call this 'knowing the properties of number'. Being able to visualise whether a number is big or small helps us to understand that sixty is bigger than sixteen. Knowing the properties of number makes it easier to begin doing basic sums.

If a dyslexic child has poor number sense, even a

simple equation like **87 – 80** will be really hard. She might start counting backwards from **87**, right down to **7**. This is because she's unable to see that **87** and **80** are similar-sized numbers. She won't realise that it would be quicker to find the difference between the two numbers.

The English in maths

Another reason many dyslexic children have a hard time getting to grips with basic sums is because of the way schools teach maths. Maths and English may seem completely different to parents, but actually, the two subjects require similar skills.

For one thing, after the age of six, maths involves a lot of reading. The concepts in maths might be non-verbal, but we use language to talk about them! Every maths textbook or maths exam is filled with words. If a child isn't a confident reader, she may make silly mistakes in her sums, because she hasn't read the question properly.

Children also need lots of new vocabulary words for maths class. New words like 'isosceles' and 'hypotenuse' can trip up even good spellers. For dyslexics who struggle with reading or spelling, these new vocab words just add another layer of confusion.

Mixed-up, back-to-front, upside-down

All the reading that's involved in maths is a particular

problem for dyslexic children who struggle with visual distortion, where the words (and the numbers!) on the page move, blur or swirl. To add to the confusion, many maths symbols look very similar. The symbols for different numbers and functions are often the same – only tilted or flipped over. Examples:

+ and x

– and ÷

2 and 5

6 and 9

. and ,

This means that a dyslexic child is more likely to slip up and read a symbol incorrectly, especially if she's doing lots of maths problems, one after the other. Mistaking a plus sign for a multiply sign, or a decimal point for a comma, can lead her to get a drastically wrong answer – even if she's using a calculator.

Part of the problem for dyslexic children is directionality – that is, being able to instantly tell which way is left, right, up or down. This kind of confusion about direction can lead a child to read or write numbers back-to-front or upside-down.

If she accidentally writes 6 backwards on the page, it just looks a bit odd. But if she writes it upside-down, the teacher will read it as 9 and mark it as the wrong answer.

Poor number sense can make this problem worse. If a dyslexic child doesn't 'get' that 21 is a bigger number than 12, she's more likely to mix them up.

Linking meanings to words and symbols

Just as, in reading, a dyslexic child may find it hard to link a particular sound, /eɪ/ (*ay*, as in 'lane') to a letter on the page (A), in maths, she'll also struggle to link a maths function to a symbol on the page.

The way teachers use words in maths may also pose a problem. Some maths words will already be familiar to children – but they'll mean different things. In everyday life, **power** is the stuff that makes your TV work. In maths, '3 to the **power** of 4' means that you have to do the sum **3 x 3 x 3 x 3**. The trouble is, dyslexics often have trouble attaching more than one meaning to the same word.

Worse still, in maths, several different words may be used to mean the same thing. 'Plus', 'total', 'sum', 'altogether' and the + sign can all be used to mean 'add'. For a dyslexic child, one or more of these meanings might fail to stick. So, even though she knows how to add or multiply, she'll be stumped by a question that asks for the 'sum' or 'product' of two numbers.

Weak working memory

For a dyslexic child doing maths, the root of many

problems lies in working memory – that is, being able to hold (and manipulate) a lot of information in your mind at once. The classic dyslexic moment lies in dialling a phone number (or typing in an account number), finding you've done it wrong, doing it again, and finding you've done it wrong again. Parents may spot an older dyslexic child dialling a phone number and then banging the phone down in frustration because she got the wrong number – yet again!

Misdialling phone numbers is usually the result of not being able to hold several numbers in your working memory at once. This doesn't just pose problems for using the phone – it poses problems for maths class, too.

Because a dyslexic child's working memory is weak, when she does mental arithmetic, she might only be able to hold one or two numbers in her mind. Meanwhile, a non-dyslexic child with a strong working memory might be able to hold five or six numbers in her mind.

It's not just mental arithmetic that's harder if you have a weak working memory – it's maths in general. Maths textbooks are filled with two- or three-step problems. A child must solve a sum, and then use the answer to perform another sum. However, a dyslexic child is likely to forget to do part of a two-step problem. Even if her maths skills are sharp, slip-ups like this can mean she ends up underachieving.

Trouble with spelling in numbers

Maths also involves a lot of 'spelling in numbers' (writing down a long string of numbers accurately). These numbers might appear in a textbook question or on a calculator screen, or they could be read out by a teacher. Either way, a dyslexic child's weak working memory will make it harder for her to write down a string of numbers correctly.

The same spelling errors that can plague a dyslexic child when she's writing can affect her maths, too. When writing down a series of digits, she might accidentally repeat numbers (just as she repeats letters when spelling words). She might place the comma in the wrong place or use two commas by mistake.

Facts won't 'go in'

Weak working memory can also affect how well a child's brain transfers knowledge to her long-term memory. It's often the case that a dyslexic child can do a type of maths problem one week, but the next week, she has no idea. This is a problem because schools don't tend to revisit maths material. Therefore, the teacher won't pick up on the fact that a dyslexic child hasn't retained last week's maths knowledge.

In general, schools tend to use rote learning for number facts. This involves saying something over and over again in the same way, until (the theory is) you memorise it. However, this type of rote learning doesn't work well for a dyslexic child. She might parrot the facts back to the teacher today, but the knowledge doesn't go into her long-term memory. This means her progress remains slow, which baffles parents and teachers.

Can't see connections

A big part of the problem for dyslexic children is that they find it hard to see the connections between different parts of maths. A non-dyslexic child will probably understand, without it being made explicit, that **7 x 2** is the same as **2 x 7** and the same as **7 + 7** and the same as **'double seven'**. This connection – drawn between times tables, multiplication, addition, and doubling – is obvious to a non-dyslexic child. But, for a dyslexic child, it's far from obvious.

Many dyslexic children don't automatically see the patterns that run through maths. They find it difficult to use knowledge learned in, say, geometry (e.g. a square with 5cm sides has an area of 25) and apply it to algebra (e.g. 5 squared is 25). Unless the connection is made explicit, they just can't see it.

Slow to grasp sequences

When it comes to literal number patterns in maths

(sequences involving squared or cubed numbers, for example), it's likely to take a dyslexic child much longer to understand which number comes next in the sequence.

This is because dyslexics tend to struggle with putting things in the right order (sequencing). A dyslexic child might find it so hard to 'see' the natural order of numbers that she'll even struggle to count backwards. She might have learned by rote '99–100–101', without actually understanding the order of the numbers, so counting backwards ('101–100–99') will be very hard for her. By extension, this can have an impact on her learning in all areas of maths.

Presentation on the page

Presentation may also pose a problem for a dyslexic child. The child might understand the theory behind the problem, but not how to set it out on the page. Her presentation might be very scruffy. She might not line up her decimal points or set out her sums correctly. This means she's starting at a disadvantage and she's much more likely to make mistakes.

(Scruffy presentation is a particular problem for dyslexic children with dyspraxia traits. Find out more in *Chapter 10: Movement*.)

What's more, a dyslexic child might have a hard time

figuring out how to 'read' a question on the page. You read a book left-to-right, but the same is not true with maths problems:

In column addition and subtraction, you work right-to-left. In long division, you work left-to-right. In algebra, it could be that you work left-to-right *or* right-to-left. In BODMAS (Brackets, Order, Divide, Multiply, Add, Subtract)/BIDMAS (Brackets, Indices, Divide, Multiply, Add, Subtract), you work in another way altogether.

In most cases, with maths problems, if you work the wrong way, you get the wrong answer. Dyslexic children already struggle with left/right confusion in a way that non-dyslexic children do not. And this confusion is only made worse by the fact that there's no consistent rule for working left-to-right (or right-to-left) in maths.

The dyscalculia debate

Dyslexia and maths intersect in many different ways. But wait a minute ... how does 'dyscalculia' fit into the puzzle? Parents who have heard this term often assume that dyscalculia is 'like dyslexia, but with maths'. This seems like common sense, but actually, the situation is a bit more complicated.

The thing is, 'dyslexia with maths' is just ... dyslexia! We might hear more chatter about how dyslexia affects reading and writing, but it also affects maths. In fact, for some dyslexic children, maths is their biggest bugbear. They've 'muddled through' learning to read and write, but maths remains the sticking point.

Dyscalculia (literally: difficulty with counting) is a separate learning difficulty and one that's much 'newer'. Dyslexia has been studied for more than a hundred years, but dyscalculia was only officially recognised by the British government in 2001. We know much less about dyscalculia, and there's still a lot of debate about what exactly it is. Severe 'number blindness'? A broader problem with numeracy? In fact, there is no single definition yet, and the debate about dyscalculia rages on.

In practice, the diagnosis of dyscalculia is usually only given if the child has problems with maths, but no difficulties with reading and writing. However, it's important to note that some children are very good at masking their dyslexia in some areas. If a child has a natural interest in words, she may have worked extra hard to improve her reading, so that she no longer 'seems' dyslexic.

Different subject, same weaknesses

Indeed, in maths, we see repeated many of the same dyslexic weaknesses that make reading, writing, and spelling hard work. Left/right confusion, weak working memory, and problems with sequencing can all have an impact on maths work. Yet maths may be the place where we see the biggest difference between individual dyslexic children.

Some children, like Freddie (see case study), are barely held back by their dyslexia in maths class. Due to the non-verbal reasoning involved, they use maths as a refuge from language-based subjects. Other children, like Mohammed (see case study), have just a few weak areas. Many more, like Tia (see case study), find it tough to even master the basics of maths. Could a child like Tia be dyscalculic? Perhaps. However, whether you call it dyslexia or dyscalculia, the ways to support your child's maths difficulties are exactly the same.

Maths – Key Signs of Dyslexia:

- Child has trouble with times tables and number bonds
- Counts on her fingers (at an age when her peers don't)
- Makes wild guesses at answers
- Uses pen and paper for simple questions
- Uses complicated means to do 'easy' sums
- Mixes up similar symbols, like + and x
- Writes numbers back-to-front or upside-down (at a younger age)
- Makes mistakes when writing down long numbers
- Learns a maths skill easily, but then can't remember it a week later
- Only does part of a two-step problem
- Finds sequences difficult
- Struggles with written methods, because she starts at the wrong end of a sum
- Scruffy presentation

Case study: Tia and the fear (part 1)

When she was given maths homework, Tia was scared to even start.

She knew she was terrible at maths. She got the lowest mark in the class on every test. Even the simplest things, she couldn't do. In order to solve **10 + 2**, she had to count to ten on her fingers first. At home, when she played board games, she had to stop and count the number of dots on the dice when it was her turn.

When she couldn't do her maths homework, Tia's dad shouted at her. Tia's mum was more understanding – maybe *too* understanding. She always ended up giving Tia the answers.

In school, Tia fell further and further behind. The classroom assistant spent all her time helping Tia, spoon-feeding her every answer. Eventually, Tia stopped even trying to do maths by herself.

If she didn't try, she couldn't fail, so there was nothing to fear.

Case study: Freddie and the click-click-click (part 1)

Freddie loved maths.

His teacher said it was because he had strong non-verbal reasoning skills. Freddie thought it was just because maths made *sense*. In maths class, his brain went click-click-click and he *got* it.

Freddie loved maths, but he hated exams.

His teacher was always disappointed with his results. 'You made silly mistakes,' he told Freddie with a frown. 'Read the question next time.'

Freddie *had* read the question. He swore he had.

Yet, somehow, the more words the exam contained, the worse Freddie did.

Case study: Mohammed and his times tables (part 1)

Mohammed knew his times tables. After two years spent on an after-school rote learning course, he knew his times tables totally and completely.

Mohammed did so many extra hours of work per week that his parents couldn't understand why he wasn't improving in school.

Mohammed didn't *hate* maths, but he began to dread maths class all the same. He worked so hard, and yet he never did very well when it came to end-of-year exams. His teachers were baffled by his poor results. Mohammed knew his times tables – so why did he struggle with an easy sum like **18 ÷ 3**?

SUPPORTING DYSLEXIA

Filling in the gaps

Even though children like Tia, Freddie, and Mohammed are working at very different maths levels, the thing they all have in common is that they've missed out on certain fundamentals. Number bonds, times tables, odds and evens, doubles and halves – these number facts are the building blocks of maths. Yet, if a child doesn't understand a particular number fact, she'll spend a lot of time 'muddling through', rather than really learning.

It's important to find out where the gaps in your child's maths learning lie. In some cases, it will be just a few number facts that are missing. In other cases, most or *all* of the number facts aren't there. Either way, once you begin to 'fill in the gaps', your child can really start to make progress.

Stop rote learning

Number facts are essential for maths, but learning them by rote simply won't work for most dyslexic children. Repeating a number fact over and over again in the same way doesn't help a dyslexic child, because of her weak working memory.

Instead, dyslexic children need multi-sensory learning. Appealing to sight, sound, taste, smell, and touch helps number facts to really stick in their long-term memory.

Multi-sensory learning might mean tracing times tables in the bath water, singing the number bonds in the form of a song, or making bread in the shape of an isosceles triangle.

Learning a fact in a range of different ways, using all the different senses, allows your child to begin making connections and using maths ideas in different contexts. It's also a lot more fun than dreary rote learning!

Regular check-ups

Once your child begins filling in the gaps, it's important to make sure those gaps *stay* filled in. A dyslexic child will have a hard time transferring number facts into her long-term memory. So she'll need to go back over things she learned last week, last month, or even last year.

These regular check-ups help to make sure your child stays on track with her maths. If an older child seems to be falling behind, it's worth going back over the 'easy' stuff, because her learned number facts may have become rusty.

Recapping maths facts again and again really helps dyslexic children. And there's no need for it to be a drag. Why not play a fun maths game once in a while, to make sure she still remembers her times tables?

'Doing' maths!

Dyslexic children tend to learn better by *doing* than by sitting at a desk. Make maths into something that you *do*, by using props like wooden blocks, a jar of beads, or a bowl of sweets or raisins. Through practical play, help your child to see that 'divided by' simply means 'shared between' (demonstrated by sharing out beads), and 'add' simply means 'add on another building block'.

Using physical props also helps your child to build up a sense of number and develop a visual model for maths in her head. Ask your child to build one tower using three wooden blocks and then build another tower using nine blocks. Immediately, she'll be able to see that nine is a bigger number than three, because it makes a taller tower!

Clearly laid-out work

Using blocks, beads, or anything else you have around the house, makes it less painful to start solving maths problems. However, when it is time to start writing out maths work on paper, neat presentation makes all the difference.

Encouraging good habits, like clearly laid-out, step-by-step sums, will stop your child from getting mixed up. Using squared paper, with one digit in each box, makes it much easier to line up numbers. This reduces the chance of your child making mistakes.

Quite often, you'll find that the hand-outs and homework your child gets from school aren't clearly laid-out. Everything's bunched up together on the page, and the question numbers fight for space alongside the sums. All of this makes solving the problems harder. If this is the case, encourage your child to neatly copy out every question on to a separate sheet of paper, so that she won't get confused as she begins to solve the problems.

Making connections clear

A dyslexic child will probably need particular help to understand the connections within maths. So don't expect your child to automatically make links between maths concepts. She'll probably need to have these connections clearly explained to her. When it comes to different ways of describing the same sum (e.g. 'double' is the same as 'times two') talk it through with your child. Make sure she understands all the different words that might be used to mean the same thing. Talk through new vocabulary words, as well – don't expect her to 'just pick them up'.

Talking things through is also vital when helping your child with counting. This is an area where confusion commonly arises for dyslexic children. Why do we say 'sixty', 'seventy', 'eighty' and 'ninety', but not 'twoty' (for 20) or 'threety' (for 30)? Why aren't the numbers 1–13 pronounced 'onety' (10), 'onety-one' (11), 'onety-two' (12), 'onety-three' (13)? Since 'sixteen' starts with a six, why isn't it written 61? The language of counting can be contradictory, so it's important to make sure your child grasps when counting follows the rules – and when it doesn't.

Confusing counting patterns and dreary rote learning – no wonder maths has a reputation for being boring. In school, it can be. So, when parents try to help their children with maths at home, they often fall into the same old boring school routine. These traditional school methods usually don't work for dyslexic children, though. Instead, parents should feel free to bring play back into maths. Using activities, practical play, and plain old silliness can really help a dyslexic child to build up good number basics and strengthen her weak areas in maths.

MATHS – KEY SUPPORT FOR DYSLEXIA:

- Find out which number facts your child has missed out on
- Go back over old material regularly
- Ditch the rote learning
- Repeat maths facts in different ways by appealing to the senses
- Make learning physical, using blocks and beads
- Encourage good presentation, using squared paper
- Talk through the connections between different areas of maths

Case study: Tia and the fear (part 2)

Tia's parents began playing lots of maths games with Tia after school. They helped her to build up her knowledge of number bonds, times tables, and all the other basic maths skills that she'd never quite got her head around before.

When it came to homework, Tia's mum stopped giving her the answers and her dad stopped shouting at her. Instead, they encouraged her to start trying to find the answers herself.

Little by little, Tia's maths improved – and the fear went away.

Case study: Freddie and the click-click-click (part 2)

Freddie was so bright and such a keen reader of books in his spare time that it never occurred to his teachers that he might be dyslexic.

However, his parents took him for a dyslexia assessment and, to their surprise, found out that he had mild dyslexia. The official diagnosis meant that Freddie was allowed extra time in his exams. His parents worked with him to make sure that, in maths exams, he read every word-based problem slowly and carefully.

Now Freddie's maths grades match his ability.

Case study: Mohammed and his times tables (part 2)

Mohammed's parents realised that the rote learning course wasn't helping their son. Instead, they found a personal tutor who understood dyslexia. The tutor helped Mohammed to begin seeing the connections between number facts like times tables. Suddenly, learning made sense to Mohammed. He still did hours of work, but this time, it actually helped.

Now Mohammed not only knows that **six threes are 18**, he also knows that **18 ÷ 3 = 6** and **18 ÷ 6 = 3**. He knows that **18 is half of 36** and **double 9**. He now has a real feel for numbers and, best of all, he knows that his parents are proud of him.

10.

MOVEMENT

'I think dyslexia is a kind of privilege, because it helps you to see differently.'

— DAVID BAILEY (dyslexic-dyspraxic photographer)

Photographer for Vogue *and* Vanity Fair, *with exhibitions in the National Portrait Gallery and the V&A Museum*

DYSLEXIA AFFECTS DIFFERENT CHILDREN IN DIFFERENT WAYS, and movement is perhaps the area where we see the greatest difference. A dyslexic child might be a great athlete – or he might struggle to even pour a glass of juice without spilling it.

SIGNS OF DYSLEXIA

Dyslexia and dyspraxia

Many dyslexic children have no physical problems at all. Yet many others have difficulty with movement – a condition called dyspraxia or Developmental Coordination Disorder (DCD). (The two terms technically mean slightly different things: DCD is an overarching term for motor-based difficulties, while dyspraxia, a sensory-based difficulty, is actually just one specific type of DCD. However, the two terms are often merged, with 'dyspraxia' commonly used to describe both conditions.)

Dyslexia often overlaps with dyspraxia. In fact, dyslexia and dyspraxia are so closely linked that many assessors still use dyspraxia symptoms (trouble learning to tie your shoelaces, for example) to diagnose dyslexia.

Everyday clumsiness

A dyslexic-dyspraxic child will have trouble getting his body to do what he wants it to do. Dyspraxia used to be called 'clumsy child syndrome'. This is a very limited definition (and not a very kind one!), but it does contain a grain of truth.

Children with dyspraxia traits are more likely to trip over, bump into things, spill drinks, or drop what they're holding. Everyone's clumsy from time to time (especially teenagers going through growth spurts), but dyspraxic children are clumsy *all* the time.

Dyspraxia traits show themselves much earlier than dyslexia traits. You can't clearly spot dyslexia until a child begins learning to read and write, but dyspraxia can often be spotted when a child learns to crawl.

In fact, a dyspraxic child might not crawl at all – he'll start to walk! It makes sense for a non-dyspraxic child to learn to crawl and then work his way up to walking. But, for a dyspraxic child, it's not that simple, because crawling is so hard.

Crawling means coordinating two arms and two legs, so that they work together. It's this coordination that is really hard for a dyspraxic child. It's actually easier for some dyspraxic children to walk, because they only have to coordinate two legs.

Disconnect between body and brain

Coordination issues stay with dyspraxic children as they grow up. A child with severe dyspraxia might walk or run with a strange gait, as he struggles to make his legs work together. A child with mild dyspraxia might walk perfectly well, but he'll have problems with some sports.

It's not that there's anything wrong with the dyspraxic child's muscles. The problem is that his brain has trouble communicating with the muscles. In some cases, the brain may struggle to process all the sensory information coming from the body, so it will have trouble reacting to what it sees, hears, and feels. In other cases, the brain will struggle to tell the muscles what to do, so the body will move awkwardly.

Balance and posture

This disconnect between body and brain doesn't just affect coordination. It also affects balance, posture, stability, and dexterity. A dyspraxic child may struggle to sit still for an extended period. It's not that he's hyperactive and filled with lots of energy, like a child with ADHD. It's simply that he finds it much harder to fix his body and remain stable.

If a child is sitting in a chair without good support (i.e. no arm rests), or sitting cross-legged on the floor, he might 'fidget', as he tries to find a position where his body feels stable. He might slump, grab on to the table with both hands, or lean on the table. Obviously, it can be very distracting for a child in class, when sitting means constantly being close to falling over. As a result, the child will have less energy to devote to his classwork.

Chewing and talking

Sitting in a chair requires use of gross motor skills. These skills are also used to ride a bike, swim beyond a basic level, and play certain sports. However, dyspraxia also affects fine motor skills. This is where the small muscles in our hands, feet, and face have to work together in a skilled way.

Being a messy eater or mumbling when you speak may not seem like problems related to dyspraxia. But, in fact, dyspraxia can make it harder for a child to coordinate the muscles in his face, mouth, and tongue. This is called verbal dyspraxia or oral motor dyspraxia. The result is that the child may find it harder to chew his food cleanly, or even to speak clearly.

Handwriting

Other fine motor skills that we use on a daily basis involve the hands. Fine motor skills allow us to cut out a shape using scissors, tie our shoelaces, button a shirt, and produce neat handwriting.

When he writes by hand, a dyspraxic child's letters might be all different sizes, many of them formed incorrectly. He might press much too hard with his pen. He might even bend his fingers in the wrong direction, or use his thumb to lock his fingers into place, in an attempt to get a good grip on the pen.

A young dyspraxic child might find handwriting and

other fine motor skills so frustrating that he'll keep switching hands in the hope that it will be easier with the other hand. If a child doesn't 'choose' a hand until later than his classmates, this could be a sign of dyspraxia (although not all ambidextrous children are dyspraxic).

It's not just his writing that could be untidy. The way he sets out his work could be haphazard, too. He might struggle to keep his writing on the lines. He might leave too little space for the margins, or too much space for the margins. When asked to draw a picture, he might draw it in what seems like a strange place – in a corner or at the bottom of the page.

Spatial awareness

Problems with 'setting out' tend to stem from poor visual perception or poor spatial awareness. Dyspraxic children don't have a good grasp of the relationship between themselves and the objects and space that surround them.

Spatial awareness is how we anchor ourselves. When we sit on the sofa, we're aware of how far away the coffee table is, without getting out a tape measure and measuring the distance. If there's a drink on the table, we can reach for it without looking directly at it. Our senses feed information to our brain, letting us build up a mental map of where everything around us lies.

However, a dyspraxic child's spatial awareness map might be a little bit 'off'. He's more likely to misjudge the distance between himself and the coffee table – and he might accidentally knock over the drink!

Spillages and accidents are a fact of life for children with dyspraxia. As well as his problems with spatial awareness, he's likely to use too much force when reaching for an object. Because of the disconnect between body and brain, he may not be getting good feedback from his senses about what's going on around him. This means he can't judge how much force to use when picking up or putting down an object ...

Smash!

... Oops.

Over-sensitive or under-sensitive

Poor sensory feedback may also mean that the child doesn't feel how cold or hot the temperature is, so he wanders around in a T-shirt in January! On the flip side, he may also be *over*-sensitive to sensations like taste, smell or touch. For example, he may hate the feel of certain fabrics on his skin.

Parents should bear in mind that, in this area, there is often an overlap between dyspraxia and other conditions.

Over- or under-sensitivity to sensations can also be a sign of Sensory Processing Disorder or a trait of Autism Spectrum Disorder. (Find out more about ASD in *Chapter 15: Co-occurring Conditions.*)

Left/right confusion

Another theme that runs through dyslexia and dyspraxia is momentary confusion about direction. Say 'turn right here' to a non-dyslexic child and he'll turn right without even thinking about it. However, a dyslexic child might turn left instead. Even if he turns right, he might have to check himself: 'This is the correct way, isn't it?'

For a dyslexic child, it can be hard to make a split-second judgement about which way is left or right (or up or down, above or below). It is likely that this confusion about direction stems from poor spatial awareness. For him, it's harder to instantly figure out where he is in relation to the things around him.

Carrying out a series of actions

Motor planning also plays a big role in dyspraxic struggles. This is the term for carrying out a series of physical actions, in order. Our daily lives are filled with motor planning. When we get dressed, we have to put on our clothes in the right order. When we make breakfast, we have to set out a glass before we can pour juice into it.

However, dyspraxic children struggle with sequencing (putting things in the right order). For a child with dyspraxia, motor sequences aren't usually automatic. To carry out these actions, the child has to actively *think* about the sequence. If he's not devoting enough of his brain to what his body is doing, he might get out of sync.

An extreme example of motor-planning difficulty would be a child who puts on his jumper before his shirt. However, a child with mild dyspraxia is more likely to struggle to carry out a *new* series of actions: learning to bounce and then hit the ball in tennis, for example.

Getting lost

Parents are often surprised that dyspraxia might be the reason their child keeps getting lost. In fact, in order to find our way, we use both motor planning and spatial awareness.

A dyspraxic child will have trouble judging distances and figuring out where he is in relation to his surroundings, because of his poor spatial awareness. He'll also struggle to put the stages of his journey into the right order, due to poor motor planning. Confusion about directionality may mean that, even when guided by instructions, he'll *still* get lost!

A dyspraxic child may learn one particular route (around his school, for example), and then have to stick to it forever. He won't be able to orient himself well enough to build up a mental map of the school. He may also have trouble reversing journeys in his mind. So, even if he knows the way from the sports hall to the science block, he may struggle to figure out the way *back* from the science block to the sports hall.

Multi-tasking

A dyslexic child with dyspraxic tendencies might not get lost every day – just on stressful days. He might only struggle with his handwriting during exams. His coordination might get worse only when his P.E. teacher is shouting instructions at him.

It's likely that he'll struggle most when he is under pressure or trying to do several things at once. Weak working memory makes it harder for dyslexic children to multi-task. When this is combined with dyspraxic weaknesses, his gross and fine motor skills may deteriorate if his focus is divided. This is why a child's handwriting might be neat during handwriting practice, but erratic during a free-writing assignment. When he has to concentrate on more than just holding his pen correctly, his working memory gets overloaded.

At the other end of the spectrum

Many dyslexic children, like Patrick (see case study), will

struggle with dyspraxic tendencies. However, it's important to remember that many more dyslexic children won't have any physical difficulties. For children like Laura (see case study), sports may become a source of self-esteem. While other parts of school may be taxing, P.E. class will be a huge relief.

Most of the dyslexic weaknesses that affect reading and writing don't matter a jot on the sports field. So a dyslexic child might pour all of his energy into sports or physical activities, instead of battling through a homework assignment that may take him hours.

In fact, many Olympians and top-level athletes have dyslexia, including rower Steve Redgrave, figure skater Meryl Davis, cyclist Chris Boardman, racing driver Jackie Stewart, boxer Muhammad Ali, rugby player Kenny Logan, and golfer J.B. Holmes. You'll also find dyslexics at the barre: Darcey Bussell only began dancing because dyslexia made her school lessons 'so horribly difficult'. Now she's considered one of the greatest British ballerinas of all time.

Creative problem solving on the sports field

Some movers and shakers even say that dyslexia gives them an advantage. Dyslexia is sometimes linked to enhanced visuo-spatial skills. This means someone with dyslexia may have a very advanced 'mind's eye'. His visuo-spatial abilities act like a computer graphics program in his mind, allowing him to imagine in 3D.

This means that a dyslexic athlete may be able to suss out his next move by using his mind to 3D-model the sports field in the same way that he'd use a computer program. Jackie Stewart says his dyslexia allowed him to visualise every lap, every gear change, every braking distance on the race track. Wow! (Find out more in *Chapter 14: Problem Solving*.)

Yet, for every budding racing driver, there's a child who won't even try in P.E. class, for fear of making a fool of himself. The ways in which dyslexia and movement intersect can be complicated. This makes it even more important to get to grips with how your child moves, balances, and feels sensation.

MOVEMENT – KEY SIGNS OF DYSPRAXIA:

- Child began walking at a very young age (or else much later than is typical)
- Took a long time to 'choose' a dominant hand
- Clumsy
- Poor at many sports
- Haphazard handwriting
- Uncomfortable pencil grip
- Can't sit still (especially when cross-legged on the floor)
- Gets lost frequently
- (Remember: not all dyslexics have dyspraxia traits.)

Case study: Laura and the medals (part 1)

Laura's bedroom was filled with medals and trophies – and she kept winning more and more.

Laura competed at a gymnastics competition almost every weekend. For the rest of the week, she lived in the gym, training new and difficult tricks. She loved gymnastics. She loved seeing the smile on her coach's face when she stuck the landing; she loved knowing that she was good at something.

Plus, when she was at the gym, she didn't have to think about school. Laura hated school, where every assignment took her *hours* and her teachers only ever frowned at her.

Case study: Patrick and the lost tennis balls (part 1)

When Patrick played tennis in his garden, the match never lasted very long.

People had been trying to teach Patrick to play tennis for most of his life, but it was never any good. Nine times out of ten, Patrick swung his racquet but missed the ball. If he ever did hit the ball, he hit it so enthusiastically that it sailed all the way out of the garden, over the hedge, and into the road.

That's why matches with Patrick never lasted long. He usually just sat out and watched his friends play.

His PE teacher said he just didn't try hard enough. His friends laughed and said he was *pants*. His mum shrugged and said, 'That's just Patrick.'

Patrick was the boy who always had a bruise on his leg and never knew where it came from. He was the boy who dropped plates and spilled milk and, of course, always managed to lose the tennis ball.

SUPPORTING DYSLEXIA

Breaking the vicious cycle

Just like a dyslexic child, who finds reading hard and therefore refuses to read, falling further and further behind in his reading, a dyspraxic child may fall into a similar vicious cycle. A poorly coordinated child, like Patrick, won't be naturally good at sports, so he'll refuse to take part. This means he'll never build up muscles or learn physical skills. Without muscles and skills, even the simplest of physical activities will be harder for him. This is the vicious cycle of dyspraxia.

Just because a child has a weak area doesn't mean he can't strengthen that weakness. Just as practice and over-learning can help a child to strengthen his reading, writing, and maths abilities, a child with dyspraxia can improve his coordination by doing lots of exercise and strengthening his motor skills.

Getting out there and working your muscles is the key to breaking the vicious cycle of dyspraxia. A dyspraxic child may never be the star of the football team. But, with the right support, he can become more coordinated, less clumsy – and perhaps even find a sport he loves.

Getting professional advice

If you suspect your child is dyspraxic, your first port of call should be to your GP. The GP will then be able to refer your child to an Occupational Therapist to begin the diagnosis process. Children diagnosed with severe dyspraxia can get NHS-funded care from either an Occupational Therapist (OT) or a Physiotherapist.

Sessions with a professional can help a dyspraxic child to improve his coordination, balance, and dexterity. Physiotherapists deal with gross motor skills. They will help your child to strengthen his muscles, build up stability, and improve fluidity when walking. Occupational Therapists, meanwhile, carry out a similar function, but they tend to take a wider view of dealing with dyspraxia. An OT might assess your child's skill level, help him to cope better with everyday activities, and give guidance on how his school can make things easier for him.

Unfortunately, because NHS funding in this area is very narrow, only the most severe cases of dyspraxia may be able to receive free care. However, even if your child doesn't qualify, it's worth considering paying for private sessions. Occupational Therapy can be a huge help, even for a child with mild dyspraxia. As few as six sessions with a professional can make an enormous difference to a dyspraxic child's life.

Balance Boards

Often, an OT or Physiotherapist will give the child specific exercises to do, involving a Balance Board or Wobble Board. 'Rocker' Balance Boards look a bit like a see-saw, with a rectangular piece of wood or plastic balanced over a separate cylinder. You put one foot on either side of the wood and try to balance. Round Balance Boards move in all directions. They are, quite literally, a round board balanced on top of a ball.

Balance Boards can be bought from sports shops, department stores, and even supermarkets. They're popular with many athletes who want to improve their balance and core strength. They're also good for dyspraxic children, because doing Balance Board exercises helps to strengthen the muscles in the mid-section, improving posture and body awareness.

What's more, balancing on a Balance Board while doing other things (throwing pennies into a can, or passing a bean bag from one hand to the other) can help a dyspraxic child learn to multi-task better.

Things to do at home

Getting the advice of a professional is best, and Balance Boards can be a great tool, but there are plenty of other things that parents can do with their child at home. Any kind of exercise that involves coordination will help a dyspraxic child, including walking, cycling, and swimming.

The biggest problem might be encouraging a reluctant child (one who has always had trouble in P.E. class) to take part in sports, when he fears he might not measure up. Taking a free-form approach to sports, where the emphasis is on doing it in your own way (rather than the same way as everyone else), may suit a dyspraxic child better.

Children with dyspraxia also tend to prefer solo sports, such as running or swimming, because there's less pressure to perform as part of a team. If your child takes up a solo sport, encourage him to time himself each time he runs or swims. This way, he's competing against himself: 'Yes! I beat last week's time!' It can be a boost to his self-esteem, plus motivation to keep going.

Sports that give physical feedback

Traditional sports shouldn't be seen as off limits to dyspraxic children. However, it's important to understand your child's weak areas in sports. A dyspraxic child is more likely to excel at a sport where he can get physical feedback. This physical feedback might come from sports equipment (a rowing oar, or a gymnastics pommel horse), or from close contact with another person (such as in judo combat) or even an animal (in horse-riding).

Ball games *do not* typically give physical feedback. When hitting a tennis ball, a child has to rely on hand-eye coordination, spatial awareness, and good technique, in order to make sure he hits the ball correctly. He won't know if there's a problem with his swing until it's too late (the ball flies off in the wrong direction, or it falls on the ground). However, in a sport that involves physical feedback (such as horse-riding or rowing), a dyspraxic child can feel what he's doing every step of the way and make corrections, without relying on innate coordination or spatial awareness.

Suggested sports

Suggested sports and activities for dyspraxic children include:

Judo

In judo, your child can get physical feedback from his grappling partner. Plus, learning self-defence can be a big confidence-booster for any child.

Hiking (and orienteering or geocaching)

Hiking is a great way to combine exercise with getting in touch with nature. Although, your child may be more easily persuaded by the fun of orienteering or modern treasure-hunting (geocaching).

Horse-riding

The horse provides physical feedback, helping your child to readjust his movements while riding.

Obstacle courses

An obstacle course in the back garden, with ropes to climb, nets to crawl under, and cones to weave around, can help your child to improve his balance and dexterity. (This could even become prep for a stint in the Army Reserve!)

Rowing

Rowing requires strength and rhythm, but because it's very repetitive, your child won't be caught out by the unexpected.

Rugby

There's little skill or coordination needed for basic rugby (or tag rugby), but rough-and-tumble kids will enjoy getting muddy on the rugby field.

Running

All you need is a pair of trainers for running and you're set. To motivate your child, why not take part in a local fun run to raise money for charity?

Swimming

Swimming is considered one of the best sports to try, because it works your whole body, but it's low-impact.

Other suggested sports: fencing, gymnastics, cycling.

Getting the coach involved

When it comes to sports, be mindful of the fact that a dyspraxic child may need to be coached in a slightly different way from his peers. Since he may not be completely aware of what his body is doing, he may find it harder to learn a new movement just by looking and listening.

Dyspraxic children benefit from being involved in a physical demonstration. The coach may need to guide the child's arm, in order for him to understand how to carry out a particular movement. Patience and a hands-on approach are usually needed when coaching a dyspraxic child. Parents should make sure their child's coach is aware of the common weak areas of dyspraxia.

Improving fine motor skills

Strengthening gross motor skills through sports is important, but just as important is strengthening fine motor skills. These skills are needed for writing, cutting, and tying shoelaces – and they also help to support and refine gross motor movement.

There are lots of things children can do at home to improve their fine motor skills. Performing hand exercises with putty can build up the muscles in the hands. Specially developed putty is available in different grades of firmness: start with soft putty, and let your child work his way up to playing with harder putty, as his muscles develop.

Get crafty

What's more, all sorts of craft stuff can be used to build up the hand muscles: modelling clay, papier-mâché, even popping bubble wrap! Any activity where the child is using his hands to bend, crush, weave or knead a material will improve his fine motor skills. Give particular focus to activities involving pincer grip (where the index finger and thumb squeeze together to pick up an object), such as stringing beads to form jewellery or decorations.

Cutting out shapes, making collages and, generally, having (supervised) fun with scissors will also strengthen your child's hand muscles. Using scissors requires the same type of grip needed for handwriting, making it an important stepping stone to good pencil grip. Remember: if your child is left-handed, he needs left-handed scissors. (Don't be taken in by the marketing of ambidextrous scissors!) In the long run, building up the muscles in his hands will make it easier for him to control his pen when he's writing.

Handwriting help

Of course, in order for a child with dyspraxia to improve his handwriting, lots of handwriting practice will be needed. First things first: the child has to hold his pen properly. It's very important to correct bad pen grip – no matter how long he's been holding his pen in that way.

There are three efficient ways to hold a pen or pencil: 'tripod grasp' (where the thumb, index finger, and middle finger work together); 'quadripod grasp' (using thumb, index finger, middle finger, and fourth finger); 'adapted tripod' (where the pen rests between the index finger and middle finger).

However, the ideal type of grasp is the 'dynamic tripod' – a variant of the classic tripod grasp, where the thumb, index finger, and middle finger form a tripod, and there is a nice 'o' shape formed by the webbing between the thumb and index finger. The hand should be relaxed (not in a fist) with all five fingers bent slightly. While not everyone holds their pen in the same way, it's important that it is held with both sufficient control and in a manner that's pain-free.

Check your child's pencil grip by using the Owl test: the thumbnail and the index fingernail of the child's hand are the eyes and the pen nib is the beak. Parents can even attach sticky owl eyes to the child's fingernails to encourage the proper grip! *Twit twhoo!*

Support grips (pieces of plastic that slip over a pen or pencil) are also available, to help your child to keep his fingers in the right positions. For a child who presses too hard on the paper as he writes, using a light-up pen can help. Ideally, the light on the pen should flicker as he writes. (No light means he's pressing too lightly; a constant light means he's pressing too hard.)

When your child writes, also check that he is angling his paper correctly. The paper should be angled 30–40 degrees anticlockwise, if he's right-handed, or 30–40 degrees clockwise, if he's left-handed. The other hand should be used to stabilise the paper.

Sitting properly

When a dyspraxic child is writing or doing any kind of schoolwork, it's important to make sure that he's sitting properly. Whether he's aware of it or not, your child will be distracted if he's uncomfortable in his chair. This is true for all children, but it's especially the case for dyspraxic children, who have trouble with balance. He might be concentrating so hard on sitting upright that he can't focus on his work!

Ideally, when he's sitting, your child's feet should be flat against the floor. If the chair is too high, it's easy to buy a foot rest, or make one from a box or a phonebook.

His chair should have good back support and, ideally, arms that can be adjusted to the right height.

An angled writing board or writing slope can also be helpful for any child. These boards, which are available to buy, encourage better posture. No more hunching over a desk while working! They can also help with a dyslexic child's confusion about direction. When using an angled board, up really does mean up, and down means down.

Work-arounds

The best solutions for children with dyspraxia lie in building up motor skills and improving coordination. However, temporary work-arounds can help to make a dyspraxic child's life a little easier.

Work-arounds might mean: shoes that fasten with Velcro; curly shoelaces; T-shirts and jumpers that can be pulled on over the head; trousers with elasticated waistbands. (All save fiddling with shoelaces and buttons.) There are also 'training' or battery-operated scissors available, which make cutting easier.

Perhaps the biggest work-around is the computer. Children with dyspraxia often find typing much easier than writing by hand. Speech recognition software even makes it possible to write an essay just by talking.

Don't let your child become completely reliant on

computers or other work-arounds, though. There are still lots of situations where a child needs to be able to write by hand – or use scissors, or button a shirt. With the right support, there's absolutely no reason why a dyspraxic child can't master those skills.

MOVEMENT – KEY SUPPORT FOR DYSPRAXIA:

- Visit an Occupational Therapist or Physiotherapist
- Try Balance Board exercises
- Choose sports that give physical feedback
- In solo sports, encourage your child to time himself, in order to track progress
- Use putty to build up hand muscles
- Do crafts involving kneading, weaving, and crushing
- Work on efficient pencil grip to help with handwriting
- Make sure chairs are adjustable for stable posture
- Use angled writing boards

Case study: Laura and the medals (part 2)

When Laura was diagnosed with dyslexia, her parents began taking her to weekly sessions with a tutor. At first, Laura hated it. She hated missing gymnastics training. She hated doing more of the same school stuff that she was never any good at.

Gradually, however, the tutor began to help Laura to get better at reading and writing and maths. And Laura's parents were able to build on what the tutor taught Laura, playing games and doing activities with Laura to help with her learning.

After just a few short months, Laura has found that she dreads school much less. She still prefers doing gymnastics, but it's not just an escape route for her any more.

Case study: Patrick and the lost tennis balls (part 2)

After Patrick was diagnosed with dyspraxia, his Occupational Therapist recommended using a Balance Board.

Patrick was sceptical. *Is this a joke? I can barely stay upright on solid ground! This* has *to be a joke.*

However, Patrick's dad knew that he really wanted to try surfing. He told Patrick that all the top surfers used Balance Boards. And, if Patrick practised on his Balance Board every day, Dad promised that they could go surfing in Newquay.

Despite his scepticism, doing exercises on the Balance

Board became a new part of Patrick's daily routine. He gritted his teeth and kept at it, imagining surfing trophies and adoring crowds. He also started swimming every weekend, after the Occupational Therapist suggested it might help.

It wasn't an overnight miracle, but slowly Patrick found that his balance and coordination really did improve. Patrick knows he'll never be a Wimbledon champion, but at least now he doesn't feel embarrassed when he plays cricket, football or even tennis with his mates. What's more, all his friends are really jealous of his new surfing skills – and his upcoming trip to Newquay!

11.

TIME AND ORGANISATION

"

'I just approach problems differently. It's very easy for me to jump conceptually from A to Z.'

— **JOHN CHAMBERS (dyslexic CEO)**

CEO of Cisco Systems, Inc. and one of Time *magazine's '100 Most Influential People'*

THE PROBLEMS THAT DYSLEXIC CHILDREN ENCOUNTER WITH managing their time and staying organised are not well known and often misunderstood. If a child is tardy or forgetful, it's easy to call it laziness. But there are good reasons why a dyslexic child might be late for school or forget her gym bag.

SIGNS OF DYSLEXIA

Telling the time

Dyslexic children commonly struggle with learning to tell the time. A dyslexic child might see her classmates pick up telling the time easily. For her, meanwhile, it may end up being a much longer process.

Looking at the hands and markings of a clock face poses the first problem. Many dyslexic children struggle to immediately tell left from right, without stopping to think about it. So it's hard for them to instantly know which way to 'go round' the clock face and which hand is which.

Clock-makers don't make it easy for dyslexic children, either. Many clocks feature Roman numerals instead of numbers. This means yet another thing that a dyslexic child needs to 'decode'. Some clocks don't have any markings at all! This can leave the child completely lost, especially if her grasp of time is already shaky.

Even buying a digital clock doesn't always make things easier. In some cases, it will mask the problem, so the child will be able to pretend everything's fine. In other cases, if the child struggles with visual distortion, she'll find the numbers shift places. This makes it hard to instantly read the time, even on a digital clock.

Names and numbers

A dyslexic child may get even more confused by the way we talk about time. We don't say 'forty-five minutes past eight', we say 'quarter to nine'. We call 12 o'clock either 'noon'/'midday' or 'midnight'. Some people even talk in military time: 'it's sixteen-hundred hours!'

Dyslexic children struggle with concepts that have more than one name. Even if a child understands how to read 8:45 on a clock, she may not grasp that that's the same thing as 'quarter to nine'.

60 minutes in an hour

Telling the time also means switching to a different counting system. Here, we use 'base 60', where a unit is 60 (60 minutes in an hour; 60 seconds in a minute). Of course, this is perplexing to a child who might already have trouble in maths class, where she has learned that everything is based on 10. In both time-keeping and maths, we use the same words, 'half' and 'quarter'. But, when a child is in maths class, the words mean one thing, and when she's telling the time, they seem to mean something completely different.

What's more, a dyslexic child can't resort to 'working out' timings on paper, the way she'd do with maths sums. If a friend says, 'it's quarter to ten now – I'll meet you in

45 minutes,' how can a dyslexic child work out what time they're supposed to meet? It would be impossible for her to use column addition to work out timings – even if she had a piece of paper to hand. Base 60 practically forces the child to carry out mental arithmetic. And guess what? Because of weak working memory, dyslexic children often struggle with mental arithmetic!

Months of the year

Keeping track of the months of the year involves learning yet another unit of measurement. Here, there are 24 hours in a day, 7 days in a week, and 31 days in a month. Except when there are 30 days in a month – or 28, or even 29.

When we talk about the months of the year, we use yet more words to represent numbers. January is the first month, February is the second month, and so on. Ask a dyslexic child to tell you the months of the year and it's likely she'll reel them off with no problem, as long as she can start with January. But ask her to recite the months of the year backwards and she may be stumped.

This is an example of a dyslexic child memorising facts without really understanding them. A non-dyslexic child may find it easy to understand that the months of the year form a sequence. She can picture in her mind how each month fits into a year. However, a dyslexic child may struggle with sequencing (putting things in the right order), so her mental picture of how the months of the year fit together is likely to be fuzzy.

The concept of time

For some dyslexics, the bottom line is: they just don't *get* time. Other children develop a sense of time naturally. As they grow up, without making an effort, they begin to know how long an hour is, how long a week is. For dyslexic children, however, these ideas may remain hazy.

The problem is, children are never really taught to understand time. They're expected to 'just pick it up'. However, 'just pick it up' doesn't work for dyslexic children, who learn better if a subject is explained to them clearly and repeatedly.

Parents may notice that their dyslexic child often makes 'silly mistakes' when talking about time. The child will say 'now' when she really means 'later'. She'll say 'tomorrow' when she means 'today'.

This is another example of dyslexic struggles with 'rapid naming' (not being able to come up with the word you mean in a hurry). It's likely to be made worse by the haziness that surrounds time for dyslexics. In their minds, the meanings of words like 'today' and 'tomorrow' are weak and therefore often confused.

Losing track of time

If a child is hazy about the concept of time, it stands to reason that she will also struggle to *manage* her time. Dyslexic children often feel that they 'lose track of time'. Of course, everybody does this sometimes. If we're engrossed in something, time flies. But some dyslexic children will lose track of time *all* the time.

She may sit down to complete a task and then look up at the clock and realise that two hours have gone by and she didn't even notice! She didn't *feel* like it was two hours; the time just slipped away.

Little wonder, then, that dyslexic children also struggle with *estimating* time. They may be unable to figure out how long it will take them to do a particular task. Because a dyslexic child might not have that natural 'sense of time', she finds it hard to guess how long it will take to walk to the shops, finish her homework, or tidy her room.

Worse still, a dyslexic child is likely to *under*estimate how long a task will take. This means she usually won't leave enough time to do it. She'll end up running behind schedule – not just once in a while, but every single day.

Organisation

A dyslexic child's problems with time can be made worse by her problems with organisation. Being organised involves putting things in the right order and remembering everything you need to do. Unfortunately, both are weak areas for a dyslexic child.

In maths class, sequences pose problems for dyslexics. But we also use sequences in our everyday lives. For example, sequences help children to get ready every morning and pack their school bags with the right things. However, a dyslexic child, like Alfie (see case study), might constantly find himself leaving the house and then running back inside because he forgot something.

Excuses, excuses?

Staying organised is also made much harder by the common dyslexia trait of weak working memory. Other children can hold several pieces of information in their working memory. However, a dyslexic child can usually only hold one or two pieces of information in her mind at one time. She might have the best of intentions, but the stuff she needs to remember will simply drift out of her mind.

The classic example of this is homework. A dyslexic child might forget she was given homework. Or she might only remember part of the homework. Or she might do the homework and then leave it at home.

It's easy to be sceptical of dyslexic children's problems with time and organisation. After all, if a child is always late and never does her homework, it's natural to think that she's lazy or simply 'trying it on'. However, there's a real likelihood that it's not her fault. So it's worth making the effort to really help your dyslexic child to understand time and organisation.

> ## Note:
> Poor time management and disorganisation are often linked to dyspraxia, rather than dyslexia. However, it's the author's opinion that dyslexia traits (weak working memory, poor sequencing ability, problems with rapid naming, etc.) make time and organisation dyslexic issues, too.

TIME AND ORGANISATION – KEY SIGNS OF DYSLEXIA:

- Child has trouble telling the time
- Always late
- Mixes up time-related words
- Not able to recite the months of the year backwards
- Fails to write down homework assignments

Case study: Cherry and her shiny new watch (part 1)

Cherry loved the watch her parents bought her for Christmas. It was so pretty, with a small watch face, sparkly Roman numerals for numbers, and delicate pink hands.

However, Cherry's friends soon got tired of her showing off her new watch. Her friends would ask her for the time and, instead of telling them, she'd take off her watch and *show* them the time.

Her friends thought she was a show-off. But, the truth was, Cherry couldn't read her pretty watch. She was just too embarrassed to admit it.

Case study: Alfie and the vicious cycle (part 1)

Alfie was on the verge of getting excluded from school. He wasn't 'the bad kid'; he didn't shout or throw things or hit people. But he got into trouble for other things.

He was late to school almost every day. He never even got to the end of his street before he had to pop home to find his keys, his phone, his lunch, his sports kit … and everything else he needed for school. Alfie didn't do his homework very often, either. Even when he remembered to write down his assignments, he found he couldn't read his own handwriting. So how could he do his homework?

Alfie's teachers got tired of his lateness and lack of homework. So they gave him a lunchtime detention. The trouble was, Alfie forgot he was supposed to go to detention, so he didn't turn up. Then his teachers gave him an after-school detention. But he forgot to go to that detention, too. He just *forgot*. He really did. His teachers never believed him, though. Finally, he got so many demerits that his teachers started talking about suspension.

Case study: Zane, the technology fanatic (part 1)

Zane loved his phone and his computer and all the rest of his gadgets. He set up lots of electronic reminders, which meant that he was never late for anything and he always remembered his homework. His phone featured a big digital clock, which meant he always knew the time.

But Zane had a secret. When his friends arranged a time to meet (quarter past three or twenty to four, say), he wasn't always sure when he needed to get there. He used his trusty phone to text his mates: *what time are we meeting again?* A text usually came back, with the time in digits, which Zane could understand.

Except, sometimes his friends forgot to text him back. Rather than show up at the wrong time, Zane just stayed at home.

SUPPORTING DYSLEXIA

Back to basics

Even though time might be a naturally weak area for your dyslexic child, it's perfectly possible for her to learn to tell the time just as well as her peers. However, don't expect your child to simply 'pick up' how to tell the time. It's important to explain, step by step, how telling the time works.

Take things back to basics – but don't try to do everything at once. It's completely normal for a dyslexic child to take a bit longer to learn to tell the time. Some parents panic and push their child too fast, but this will only stress her out. Just take it one step at a time. And remember the **Rule of Ten**! A dyslexic child may need to practise a new skill ten times more than a non-dyslexic child.

Here is a good step-by-step format for teaching your child how to tell the time:

> **Step 1:** learn what 'o'clock' means
> **Step 2:** learn 'half past'
> **Step 3:** learn 'quarter past'
> **Step 4:** learn 'quarter to'
> **Step 5:** learn how steps one to four relate to each other

Step 6: learn 'five past', 'ten past', 'twenty past', 'twenty-five past'

Step 7: learn 'one minute past' and all the other times to the nearest minute for the right-hand side of the clock

Step 8: learn 'five to', 'ten to', 'twenty to' and 'twenty-five to'

Step 9: learn 'one minute to' and all the other times to the nearest minute for the left-hand side of the clock.

*(**Note:** The reason to teach step 4 so early is because this is in line with what is taught and tested in schools. However, parents may feel that learning 'quarter to' after step 7 is more natural.)*

Learning vocabulary words

Parents will also need to help their child to learn the vocabulary words needed for telling the time:

- a.m. / ante (before) meridiem (midday)
- p.m. / post (after) meridiem (midday)
- noon
- midday
- midnight

Take special care with time concepts where two or three different words are used to describe one concept.

These can be very confusing for dyslexic children. For example, 'noon', 'midday' and '12 o'clock' all mean the same thing. Words that have a different meaning when telling the time than they have in maths class (e.g. 'quarter' and 'half') should also be clearly pointed out.

Be aware that an older dyslexic child might be simply 'muddling through' telling the time. She might have mastered the basics of time, but she still doesn't understand (for example) the difference between a quarter of an hour and half an hour. Bringing your child back to basics will help to fill in the gaps in her knowledge, so that she can tell the time confidently, instantly, and in a stress-free way.

Developing a sense of time

As well as learning how to tell the time, dyslexic children also need help to develop a sense of time. As your child becomes aware of how long each unit of time lasts, she will get better at understanding and estimating time.

You could ask your child to tick off each day on her calendar, so that she's aware of how long a week or a month lasts. Some children like to have a watch that beeps every hour. This can help her to stay aware of the passing time.

Parents also have a role to play in making sure a

dyslexic child gets a true sense of time. Be very specific when you talk about time. If you say 'we're leaving in five minutes', make sure you *mean* five minutes. Parents tend to manipulate time to suit their needs. 'I'll be with you in one minute' – does that sound familiar?

Most children will understand that 'be with you in one minute' might actually mean five minutes. But, for a dyslexic child, it will add to her sense of confusion about time. It might sound pernickety, but giving a child an exact time ('we're leaving at 10 o'clock'), and sticking to it, will really help her.

Timed tasks

Timed tasks can also help to build up a good sense of time. Use buzzers, alarm clocks or hourglass sand timers to time how long it takes to do a task. This can be good practice for tests and exams, but don't just time schoolwork.

Encourage your child to time herself while she draws a cartoon or helps Dad with the washing up. Make it into a game. Ask her to estimate how long she thinks a particular task will take. Then let her time the task and check how long it took for her to complete it. Ask her to repeat the process another day and see how much her time-estimating skills improve.

Timing homework

Building up a sense of time when working on homework is also important. Talk to your child's teacher about how much time she should spend on homework. Agree upon a time limit with the teacher and stick to it. Teachers normally consider a child's concentration span to be their age in minutes, plus five.

If your child plays up while she's supposed to be doing her homework, the timer needs to go back to the beginning. As long as you are consistent, this normally only happens a handful of times. Your child will soon learn that if she works her hardest for the agreed length of time, homework tasks are quickly completed and she is free to enjoy the rest of her day. Dyslexic children may not get to the end of the piece of homework, but most teachers fully accept a parent writing a comment like: 'Sarah worked hard for the agreed twenty minutes, but only got as far as question eight – she found question five particularly hard.'

Visual timetables

Since good time-keeping may not come naturally to a dyslexic child, use tricks and clever reminders to keep her on track. If she struggles to get ready in the mornings and leave the house with everything she needs, a visual timetable may be the answer. A visual timetable shows a time of day (e.g. 7 a.m.) matched with a drawing or photograph (e.g. a picture of a person getting out of bed). This can help with getting to grips with the 24-hour clock, as well.

Sit down with your child and, together, make a colour-coded visual timetable. Younger children often like to have pictures of themselves on a visual timetable (for example, posing with their toothbrush for 'brush your teeth'). Teenagers may prefer finding pictures from the Internet (for example, using a picture of a pop star for 'practise guitar', or a picture of an animal in sports kit for 'pack P.E. kit for school').

To aid remembering, a dyslexic child can look directly at her visual timetable (which might be hung in her bedroom) and also visualise it when she's in a different room. Instead of keeping lots of words in her head, she can instead visualise the picture that shows what she needs to do next.

A simpler version of the visual timetable might be a checklist, attached to the child's key ring or backpack. The checklist (which she automatically picks up, along with her keys) might include a quick list of everything she needs to take with her to school.

Write things down

Other people may be able to rely on keeping a lot of information in their short-term memories, but dyslexics usually need to jot things down to stay organised. An older dyslexic child can keep a notebook with her and write down notes about what she needs to do. (The only trouble is, she might need daily help to remember to check what she wrote down!) This is one area where technology can be a great help. A teenager may be happiest to program her phone with reminders.

Parents of a younger dyslexic child can help her by writing reminders and lists. Post-It notes dotted around the house can work for some parents. Other parents have a white board (or several white boards!) with schedules and reminders written in big letters.

Keep at it!

It's important for parents to treat time-keeping and good organisation as things that you learn and get better at doing. It's all too easy to sigh and say, 'Well, that's just how she is!' But there's no reason why a chaotic dyslexic child can't be helped to become more punctual and well-organised.

What's more, this will have a knock-on effect for other areas of her learning. No more excuses about forgotten homework! No more being late for football practice! A great result all round.

TIME AND ORGANISATION – KEY SUPPORT FOR DYSLEXIA:

- Teach telling the time in a step-by-step way
- Make sure time-related vocab words are understood
- Try not to say 'one minute' when you mean five minutes
- Use timed tasks to help her to build up a sense of time
- Make visual timetables or checklists
- Write things down on Post-Its or white boards

Case study: Cherry and her shiny new watch (part 2)

When Cherry finally revealed that she couldn't read her pretty watch, her parents took her to the watch shop to exchange it for a different one. The watch she chose had a large face, big hands, and easy-to-read numbers. It wasn't as pretty as the sparkly pink watch, but Cherry liked it a lot more.

Cherry's dad – who'd also had trouble learning to tell the time when he was young – worked with Cherry to make sure she really understood how to read her watch. Now, when one of her friends asks the time, Cherry is the first person to shout out the answer.

Case study: Alfie and the vicious cycle (part 2)

Alfie's mum knew that Alfie wasn't lazy or naughty or a bad seed – but she needed his school to believe it, too.

She made an appointment to see the SENCo and the head teacher. When Alfie's mum explained the situation, they were surprisingly understanding. They agreed to make sure that all of Alfie's teachers wrote down Alfie's homework in his homework diary or gave him a print-off to staple into the diary. The teachers also began sending regular emails to Alfie's mum, with details of when homework assignments were due.

Every Thursday, Alfie had a meeting with his new

Learning Support Mentor. Her name was Mrs Mayer and she supported Manchester City just like Alfie. Angrily, at first, Alfie began to tell Mrs Mayer why he was always late and why he always forgot his homework. Amazingly enough, Mrs Mayer actually believed him! She didn't call him lazy or a liar.

For the first time, Alfie has stopped feeling like school is a battle that he's fighting alone. He's still forgetful and tardy sometimes, but now he feels like there are people next to him on the battlefield: his mum, Mrs Mayer, and even some of the other teachers.

Case study: Zane, the technology fanatic (part 2)

As a compensating dyslexic, Zane had got so used to muddling through with life that he refused to ask for any help.

His six-year-old sister, Ali, was *always* asking for help, though. *Zane, help me with this. Zane, help me with that.* It drove him crazy.

One Sunday, Ali demanded that he help her learn to tell the time.

'Stop bothering me,' he told her. 'Go ask Mum.'

Zane spent the afternoon playing on his phone in the living room, while his mum helped Ali learn to tell the time. Zane didn't eavesdrop exactly. They were just talking loudly. It took Ali weeks to get the hang of telling the time and, every time Mum helped her, Zane happened to be in the same room. Total coincidence.

Zane wasn't sure how it happened, but after he heard his mum explain telling the time to his sister over and over again, he slowly began to understand. One day, he looked at the big analogue clock in the living room and found that he could read it without hesitating. Telling the time was ... easy!

Zane still loves his phone and all of his other gadgets, but he doesn't have to rely on them quite so much anymore.

12.

MUSIC

"

'Dyslexia made me realise that people who say "but you can't do that" aren't actually very important. I don't take "no" too seriously.'

— **RICHARD ROGERS (dyslexic architect)**

House of Lords peer and designer of the Millennium Dome

WHEN A CHILD LEARNS TO PLAY AN INSTRUMENT, FAMILIAR dyslexic weaknesses may rear their ugly heads. However, if the child has begun to overcome his dyslexia in maths or English class, he already has a head start in his music lessons.

SIGNS OF DYSLEXIA

A gap between musical ability and progress

There's no link between dyslexia and musical ability – and no reason a dyslexic child shouldn't play any instrument he likes. However, what may happen is that a gap opens up between a child's natural musical ability and the amount of progress he makes.

If a child is sensitive to the sounds of music, but has trouble playing, sight-reading and keeping rhythm, even after many lessons, this could be a sign of hidden dyslexia.

Seeing and hearing

Learning to sight-read music can be a slower process for a dyslexic child.

Part of the problem is that learning an instrument means learning a new language. If a dyslexic child is already struggling to read English, reading foreign musical words as well can be a nightmare.

Most musical terms are Italian, so they follow different language rules from English. This makes it hard for a dyslexic child to connect what he hears his teacher say with what is written on his sheet music.

What's more, many musical terms are similar-sounding. A child that begins playing at the wrong tempo might be scolded for not paying attention. However, it could be that he simply mixed up *adagio* and *allegro*!

Visual distortion, which some dyslexic children experience as they try to read, can also cause the staves and musical notation to blur or move on the page. As a result, a dyslexic child may resist even trying to read sheet music.

Dyslexia may alter what a child sees — and what he hears, too. Poor auditory discrimination makes it harder for the child to tell the difference between similar sounds. In a musical context, it could mean that he needs to concentrate much harder to follow musical sounds and keep his own rhythm.

Handling the instrument

Playing a musical instrument requires you to keep the brain in sync with the body. Almost all instruments make use of both hands. Some, like the organ, make use of both feet, too. So playing requires well-developed fine motor skills.

If a child has dyspraxia symptoms, such as difficulty tying his shoelaces, he might also have problems handling his instrument. Making tiny, controlled movements with his fingers can be much more of an effort for a dyspraxic child.

Even for a dyslexic child with good fine motor skills, the act of playing an instrument may be harder. Dyslexics often get confused between left and right, up and down – especially when they're under pressure. Playing an instrument means being able to quickly follow instructions on which way to move your fingers (left or right, up or down) and which hand to use. If the child is working hard and concentrating on learning lots of new things, he may momentarily forget which way is which.

Music teachers can also make dyslexics' lives harder, if they're not clear with their instructions. 'Going up/down' may refer to moving your fingers up and down the instrument, *or* it could refer to going up or down in pitch!

Doing things in the wrong order

The difference between beautiful music and horrible caterwauling often comes down to doing the right things in the right order. However, dyslexic weakness with sequencing and working memory can cause children to struggle in this area.

Consider the first thing a child learns to play: scales. The child has to hold a series of notes in his working memory and then play them himself in the right order. For a child who finds it harder than most to grasp everyday patterns, mastering a musical sequence can also be tricky.

Music can be thought of as the art of multi-tasking. As well as doing everything in the right order, a musician is always doing several things at once. He has to handle the instrument with his hands (and maybe his feet, too). He has to read the sheet music. He has to listen to (and remember) his teacher's instructions. If he's playing with other musicians, he has to stay aware of what the people around him are playing – all while looking at the conductor.

Phew! It's no wonder that this level of multi-tasking can tax a dyslexic's working memory, which is generally much weaker than average.

Forgetting to practise

It stands to reason that getting better at playing a musical instrument requires a lot of practice. Yet a dyslexic child may fail to practise every day – not because he's lazy, but because he has trouble managing his time and staying organised.

His poor grasp of time means that he might *plan* to practise, but then run out of time. His weak working memory means that he might forget which piece his teacher asked him to practise. His lack of organisation means that he might even fail to bring the right sheet music and equipment with him to the lesson.

Poor time management and disorganisation may cause a child to fall further and further behind in his musical studies. It can be frustrating for parents and child alike, but it doesn't have to be like this. A musical child who's dyslexic can be supported in plenty of ways.

MUSIC – KEY SIGNS OF DYSLEXIA:

- Child seems 'musical', but makes very slow progress
- Finds it hard to read/remember musical terms
- Gets left and right mixed up while playing in pressurised situations
- Has trouble playing and listening to instructions at the same time
- Forgets to practise and/or fails to bring the right equipment

Case study: Bella and the flute (part 1)

As soon as Bella could talk, she started to sing. She sang in the bath. She sang on the way to school. She even sang at the dinner table!

Bella's musical ability was obvious. And she liked music much better than reading or writing or dreaded maths.

Her parents found a music teacher and Bella began to learn the flute. At first, she loved playing the flute. But, as the weeks turned into months, Bella didn't seem to be enjoying her lessons anymore. She never practised unless her mum nagged her and she often turned up at her lessons without her sheet music.

Eventually, the flute was left to gather dust at the bottom of Bella's wardrobe.

Case study: Harry and the piano (part 1)

Harry loved playing the piano. He loved the music and the feel of the keys against his fingers. He felt a rush of happiness every time he learned a new piece.

He wasn't as good at piano as his brother, Toby, though. Toby was on Grade 8, while Harry, just two years younger, was only on Grade 3. On the day of his Grade 4 exam, Harry was really nervous. If he failed, Toby would laugh at him.

'I want you to play a scale of C minor using your left hand,' the examiner told Harry.

Harry took a deep breath (he hated C minor) and began to play.

'No, no, no,' the examiner said. 'Your *left* hand.'

Harry turned bright red. He realised he'd been playing using his *right* hand. Harry was so flustered by his mistake that he couldn't concentrate for the rest of the exam.

SUPPORTING DYSLEXIA

Music is good for dyslexics!

The good news for parents of dyslexic children is: the natural musical ability is the part you can't teach. The rest is much easier to fix.

It's even been suggested that learning an instrument can be a big help to a dyslexic child. It gives him a new and exciting way to build up strengths in reading, organisation, rhythm, and close listening. Even basic musical training (e.g. finding the beat, clapping rhythms, learning to sing in tune) can help to improve common dyslexic weaknesses. Expensive private lessons aren't necessary, either. Try out low-cost alternatives for your child, such as a choir, bell-ringing, or drumming (perhaps as part of a samba band).

Picking a first instrument

However, if you'd like your dyslexic child to have dedicated music lessons, care should be taken in picking his first instrument. Pick the wrong instrument (one that clashes with his dyslexia) and he may get frustrated and quit. For this reason, it's best to avoid the piano – at least at first. There's no reason an older dyslexic shouldn't take up the piano, but at the beginning, he'll probably find all the multi-tasking overwhelming (using both hands and his foot, reading more than one line of music).

It's better to slowly build up a child's musical skills (reading sheet music, understanding musical terms) as he learns to play a 'straightforward' instrument, like the trombone. Then he'll be ready to take on the challenge of an instrument like the piano.

As a first pick for a musical dyslexic child, brass instruments (trombones, trumpets, tubas, etc.), saxophones, and violins are a good bet. They require only one line of music to be read, meaning there's less need for multi-tasking and less room for left/right confusion. Shortage instruments (also called endangered instruments), such as bassoons, violas, double basses, oboes, French horns (as well as trombones and tubas), are also worth considering, because there tends to be less competition from other musicians. This means there will be more encouragement and support to keep playing, in a band or orchestra setting.

Address weak areas

Learning any musical instrument requires you to use certain muscles in new and challenging ways. For a dyslexic child with dyspraxia traits, this may prove particularly difficult. If your child has problems gripping and making movements on his instrument, it may be necessary to strengthen his fine motor skills. Visiting an Occupational Therapist for expert care, or finding exercises to do with your child at home, can lead to big improvements. (*Chapter 10: Movement* has ideas for exercises to strengthen fine motor control.)

It's also a good idea to make sure that sheet music is easy on the eyes for your child. If your child has coloured overlays, make sure he uses them for his sheet music. And, even for children who don't use overlays, getting the sheet music enlarged can make a big difference. You could also highlight and colour-code the different lines and notes on the sheet music – red for E, blue for G, green for B, etc. Having a different colour for symbols that look alike (such as a quaver and a semi-quaver) may also help the child to remember which is which.

Making practice into a routine

Encourage your child to practise his instrument every day at the same time. Leaving him to 'do it whenever' may mean it never gets done. If he doesn't have a strong sense of time, you could link practice to an activity like breakfast or dinnertime. This way he knows that right after dinner, every day, he practises his instrument.

For a child who tends to forget what he needs for his music lesson, the answer might be a checklist. The checklist could be attached to his instrument case, so that every time he picks up the case, he can remember everything he needs. *Music stand? Got it! Sheet music? Got it!* ... and so on. Include pictures on the checklist for younger children.

(Of course, if your child regularly forgets his instrument altogether, more drastic measures might be needed! Try hanging a white board near the front door and writing reminders in big letters: 'Got your trombone, Jack?')

Access arrangements

Don't be surprised if your child's music teacher doesn't understand how his dyslexia affects him while he plays an instrument. Many people think of dyslexia as 'a reading thing'. Due to this misconception, it's important to make it clear to the music teacher which parts of playing the instrument are extra difficult for your child. Ask the teacher to give clear instructions and try not to get irritated if the child mixes up left and right.

When your child is ready to take music exams, make sure he gets all the special provisions to which he is entitled. Many music exam boards now make special access arrangements for children with a formal dyslexia diagnosis.

Check with the particular exam board for specifics, but usually arrangements involve extra time, optional enlarged sheet music (or use of coloured overlays) and possible use of a scribe (for written exams). Exam candidates may also be allowed extra time for sight-reading and given permission to take into the exam room their scale book, which they may glance at (for reference), but not read from. Without penalty, within reason, dyslexic candidates may also be allowed replays (of a scale) and additional attempts.

Hard work pays off

It can be tough to swallow, but a dyslexic child may need to work harder than his peers to master his instrument. He may need to do extra practice. And it might be a longer process for him to learn all the musical terms.

However, hard work in music really pays off. What's more, in learning an instrument, your child will build up strategies for dealing with his dyslexic weaknesses. This can have positive knock-on effects for other areas of his learning.

MUSIC – KEY SUPPORT FOR DYSLEXIA:

- Choose a dyslexia-friendly (first) instrument
- Improve fine motor skills with exercises
- Enlarge and colour-code the sheet music
- Encourage your child to practise at the same time every day
- Attach a checklist of must-have equipment to the instrument
- Explain dyslexic weaknesses to the music teacher
- Investigate access arrangements for music exams

Case study: Bella and the flute (part 2)

Bella had been diagnosed with dyslexia when she was just seven, but her parents assumed dyslexia only affected her reading ability. However, when they learned more about dyslexia, they began to realise that lots of Bella's problems with the flute fitted with common dyslexic weaknesses.

Bella's dad found a new flute teacher – one who was open to supporting Bella's dyslexia. At home, Bella's parents did all they could to help her: together, they colour-coded all her sheet music and drew up a checklist of equipment she needed. They also nudged her into practising every day.

With so much more support, Bella was able to rediscover just how much she loved the flute.

Case study: Harry and the piano (part 2)

Harry's parents couldn't understand why Harry failed his piano exam. Their older son, Toby, never had any problems. And, the truth was, Harry worked much harder at his piano practice than Toby did.

Harry's parents took Harry for a dyslexia assessment and found out that he had mild dyslexia. When they sat Harry down and explained that dyslexia was the reason he found the piano so hard, it was a huge relief for Harry. He wasn't stupid, after all! Best of all, Toby said that he was sorry for laughing at Harry. (Well, Toby really only mumbled the apology, but it made Harry feel good anyway.)

Harry and his parents agreed that it would be best if he took a break from the piano for a while. Instead, they bought Harry a trombone and arranged for lessons. However much Harry loved the piano, he loved the trombone even more! He found the trombone so much more straightforward and his progress was so much quicker. He even joined the school jazz band.

(It's possible that Harry's parents preferred the sound of piano practice to the sound of trombone practice, but mostly they were just happy that Harry was happy.)

13.

FOREIGN LANGUAGES

> 'My dyslexia and my challenges through school were the absolute perfect training for an expedition.'
>
> — **ANN BANCROFT (dyslexic explorer)**
>
> *First woman to trek to the North Pole*

FOR A CHILD WHO HAS ALREADY STRUGGLED WITH READING AND writing in English class, it can feel like *déjà vu* when she begins learning other languages.

SIGNS OF DYSLEXIA

Silly mistakes or slow progress

Learning modern foreign languages can open up new parts of the world to children. And they're a great asset for working life, when the child grows up. Yet dyslexic weaknesses can have a big impact when it comes to learning languages.

A dyslexic child may make silly mistakes (or crazy guesses) while reading a foreign language. She may enjoy the conversational element of learning a language, but hate to do the reading and writing parts of her homework. Alternatively, a dyslexic child may start out well in languages, but finds that her progress drops off as she reaches secondary school.

New rules, same old problems

For a child who hasn't got to grips with her English reading and spelling rules yet, learning a whole new set of language rules can seem like a nightmare. When you add in new concepts, like gendered words and accented letters, this can increase the level of confusion for dyslexic children.

Just as with reading English, reading a foreign language means connecting a symbol on the page to a sound that's spoken aloud. This requires good phonological awareness – and it's an area where dyslexic children tend to struggle. In practice, this means that a dyslexic child may read more slowly in a foreign language. She may find it harder to connect the non-English words she hears spoken aloud with the words she sees written on the page.

Indeed, a dyslexic child may not even hear the words of a foreign language correctly, due to problems with auditory discrimination. She may mix up similar sounds, or find it difficult to notice when one foreign word ends and the next one starts.

The common dyslexic weakness with rapid naming can also make language-learning harder. If the child has problems quickly coming up with the word she wants in English, this is made even harder if she's speaking in French, for example.

On-the-hoof translations

Mastering a language means a lot of 'quick thinking', using your working memory to translate words and phrases in a hurry. However, since dyslexics' working memory tends to be weaker than average, this can pose a problem. A bright dyslexic may end up underachieving in foreign language class, because her weak working memory makes quick translations so much slower.

Working memory is particularly important when it comes to writing in a foreign language. Figuring out what you want to say in an essay and putting your thoughts in order takes up a lot of memory capacity. For a dyslexic child with a weak working memory, doing these things *and* making on-the-hoof translations can lead to memory overload.

Rote learning: a pain in every language

What's more, language classes tend to rely on the type of learning techniques that don't work well for dyslexic children. The 'look and say' method – where you look at a foreign language word on the page, say it out loud, and try to memorise it – is still popular in many language classes. Yet a dyslexic child is likely to struggle with the 'look and say' method. Using phonics to break down words into their smallest parts is better for a dyslexic child, but this method of learning is rarely used in language classes.

Rote learning – repeating something over and over in the same way – is also commonly used. However, a dyslexic child, with a weak working memory, won't respond well to rote learning. This means she'll find it harder to retain the new words and language rules she needs to master a foreign language.

Some languages are trickier than others

There are basic problems that affect dyslexics when learning any language. Yet some languages may prove trickier than others for dyslexic children. In terms of reading and spelling rules, certain languages are more logical than others. Parents may be familiar with their child's complaint: 'French is so hard! It doesn't make any sense!' The thing is, your child is right: French *is* hard! It *doesn't* make sense!

French is filled with language gremlins that make speaking, reading and writing very difficult. There are lots of mute letters, where you don't say aloud the letter at the end of a word (e.g. 'choux'). Children will also have to learn the gender of objects and master accented letters.

Common problems of the English language are multiplied in French. Nobody loves homophones (sound-alike words) more than the French! Words also tend to run into one another (e.g. 's'il vous plaît'), which is a pain for children with auditory discrimination problems.

Opaque languages

French is an 'opaque' (or 'non-transparent') language. This means that, often, French words aren't written the way they're spoken. French doesn't follow a regular, consistent set of rules. So sometimes letters are pronounced one way; other times, they're pronounced a completely different way. Other examples of opaque languages include Danish and Portuguese – and English, of course!

Dyslexic children aren't alone in finding opaque languages hard work. Anyone will struggle to master so many confusing rules. But specific dyslexic weaknesses, including weak working memory and poor auditory discrimination, may put a dyslexic child at a disadvantage.

That's not to say that any foreign language is 'too hard' for a dyslexic child to learn. With the right support, your child can certainly do well in languages – yes, even in dreaded French!

FOREIGN LANGUAGES – KEY SIGNS OF DYSLEXIA:

- Child enjoys conversation in foreign languages, but hates reading and writing
- Excels at some languages, but not at others
- Reads very slowly in foreign languages
- Guesses at what words mean instead of making translations
- Mixes up similar-sounding foreign words over and over

Case study: Ruby and the *je ne sais pas* (part 1)

'What does *je ne sais pas* mean?' Ruby whispered to her friend Kayla. She kept her head low, so that the teacher wouldn't notice they were talking during class.

'I don't know!' Kayla said, scribbling furiously at her own worksheet.

'Yes, you dooooo,' Ruby whined. 'Please just tell me this one.'

'It means *I don't know*!' Kayla said.

'Oh.'

Ruby felt pretty silly. It wasn't that she *liked* copying off Kayla. She wished she was good enough at French to do the worksheet all by herself. She didn't mind the talking part of French, but the writing part was impossible. No matter how hard Ruby tried to memorise all the funny French words, none of them stuck.

It was frustrating, because Ruby knew she was clever. Oh, her mum was always nagging her about her poor spelling, but she got decent marks in every subject. Every subject except French, that is.

'Kayla,' Ruby whispered, 'what does *je ne comprends pas* mean ...?'

Case study: Leo and the brick wall (part 1)

Leo started learning German when he was in primary school and he loved it. He loved the bold, fizzing sound of words like *Schloss* and *Kugelschreiber*. He loved sending postcards to his German pen pal, Niklaus, and getting cards covered in loopy German script in return.

Leo was top of the class for languages in primary school, but when he moved up to secondary school, his place started to slip. He didn't like his new language, French, half as much as German. And, even in German class, he found he was confused. There were so many weird new grammar rules!

Niklaus continued to send him cards and letters, but Leo stopped sending anything in return. He was embarrassed by the fact that his German wasn't getting any better. It felt like everyone else in his class was learning more and more, but Leo had hit a brick wall.

SUPPORTING DYSLEXIA

Get a head start

Languages can be – and *should* be – fun. After all, you use them on holiday, and as a way to see new places and make friends from different countries. Yet, if your child's first exposure to languages is in a dreary classroom, and she has particular problems picking up the new words (due to dyslexia), it stands to reason that she won't find them much fun.

This is why it's important for parents to expose their dyslexic child to foreign languages early. Don't wait for school to start teaching languages. Start using the basics of a foreign language in the home, at an early age.

Dyslexic children usually enjoy the conversation part of languages more than the reading and writing parts. So keep languages light and casual. Just start talking! This means that, right from the start, your child will link languages with chatting and fun, instead of school and boredom.

Choosing a first foreign language

Teaching your child the basics of a language in the home means that you get to pick the first foreign language she learns. And, for a dyslexic child, this language should be a 'transparent' one.

Transparent languages are logical and consistent. They follow a clear set of rules. This will reduce confusion for a dyslexic child. Instead of getting tripped up by rules that don't make sense, she'll be able to quickly start enjoying her new language.

Spanish is considered the best language for dyslexic children to learn. It is a transparent language, so most of its words are spelled the way they sound. Spanish is also similar to English in its sound system, so it will feel familiar to your child.

Other transparent languages include Finnish, Greek, and Italian. However, these can pose other problems (a new alphabet for Greek; a completely different sound system for Italian). German, although it's less transparent, is similar to English, so dyslexic children often find it easy to learn. (More advanced levels of German may be tricky for dyslexic children, however, due to complex grammar rules and lots of compound words.)

Dealing with an opaque language

When your child starts school, she may not get a choice about which language she learns. However, if she has already learned (and enjoyed learning!) the basics of another language, she should have the confidence to persevere with whichever language she's given.

Opaque languages, like French, Danish, and Portuguese, may be harder for a dyslexic child to pick up. But they shouldn't be seen as off limits. Parents just need to be aware of potential pitfalls and give the right support.

The same methods that can help a dyslexic child to read in English can help her to read in another language. Forget the 'look and say' method. Forget rote learning. Focus instead on dyslexia-friendly learning.

Parents should use the learning method 'phonics', where each part of a word is 'sounded out', to help their child to understand the building blocks of her new language. Help your child to learn the new phonics patterns, vowel sounds, and alphabet sounds, as well as how they are changed by accented letters. Once she starts to understand how words are constructed in French, German or any other language, her progress will speed up.

Deeper understanding

Instead of memorising random foreign words, your child will do better if she has a deeper understanding of the language. Help her to understand its structure; how grammar works in this language, and how sentences are put together.

Also compare the foreign language to English. How is it different? How is it similar? Making explicit links between English and the foreign language will help your child to put new words in context.

Instead of rote learning, use multi-sensory learning to help your child to memorise the most common words of her new language. Tap into all of the five senses, going over the words in a number of different ways. The same multi-sensory strategies (songs, mnemonics, games) that help a dyslexic child to learn English can also help her to learn a foreign language.

Remember: even if your child seems to have mastered a set of foreign words, don't assume the words have gone into her long-term memory or that she will be able to access them again. Regular recaps of past material will make sure what she's learned has 'stuck'.

Fun with languages

The good news is, with multi-sensory learning, anything can be a learning resource. Stick colourful Post-It notes on objects around the house, with the foreign word for that object written on the note. (Tip: write down both the proper spelling and the phonetic spelling of each word.)

Encourage your child to get creative by drawing cartoon strips, complete with speech bubbles. Then, using the correct foreign words in the speech bubbles, she can create her own story!

Quizzes, treasure hunts, crosswords, and word searches can also help to make learning foreign words fun. Even the simplest games, such as 'I Spy' or 'I went to the market and bought ...', can be turned into languages games.

By playing to your dyslexic child's strengths, rather than her weaknesses, you can open up the world of foreign languages to her. And making the learning process fun will mean your child is more likely to persevere when things get tough.

FOREIGN LANGUAGES – KEY SUPPORT FOR DYSLEXIA:

- Don't wait for school lessons – start chatting in a foreign language early
- Choose languages carefully – Spanish makes a good 'first language'
- Break down the structure and grammar of the new language
- Look at the language's phonics patterns
- Use songs, mnemonics and games to keep recapping words

Case study: Ruby and the *je ne sais pas* (part 2)

At first, when her dad suggested they play French-themed games, Ruby was appalled. She hated doing French at school, so why would she want to do it at home?

Yet her dad sent her on treasure hunts armed with lists of French words. Together, the two of them completed French crosswords and word searches and other games. Every time they were in the car, he made her play 'I Spy' *en Français*. Ruby thought the whole thing was a bit silly, but she had to admit, she found herself copying off Kayla in French class much less often.

When the summer holidays rolled around, Ruby's family set off for their usual holiday to Brittany in France. Normally, Ruby let her parents do all the talking, but this time, when they went to restaurants, Ruby was the first one to speak. When they needed to read street signs, Ruby was the quickest to make translations. Ruby even made a new friend, Nathalie.

'*Tu aime Français*?' Nathalie asked Ruby.

'Yeah!' Ruby said. 'Uh, I mean, *oui*!'

Case study: Leo and the brick wall (part 2)

Leo's mum was surprised when Leo told her how much he hated German.

'I thought it was your favourite subject!' she said.

'No, it's rubbish.'

Leo's mum had never been any good at languages when she was a girl (*ugh, French*), but she'd always thought Leo had a real talent for them. She hated to see him so dejected. She arranged for him to start seeing a tutor for both German and French. The tutor helped Leo to really understand both languages – how all the words in German and French fitted together.

For weeks, Leo still maintained that German and especially French were 'rubbish'. But Leo's mum saw that he was suddenly writing lots of long letters to his German pen pal, Niklaus. In fact, the two of them had started writing to each other in French, too, since Niklaus was learning French at school.

One day, Leo came home from school and showed his mum a piece of his German homework. 'The teacher said it was the best in the class,' Leo said.

'I thought you told me German was rubbish,' Leo's mum said.

'Um. Well. I guess it's okay,' Leo mumbled, but he was grinning madly.

14.

PROBLEM SOLVING

> ❝ ❞
>
> 'I don't think of dyslexia as a deficiency. It's like having CAD [computer-aided design] in your brain.'
> — **WILLIAM DREYER (dyslexic inventor)**
> *Professor of Biology and inventor of a protein-sequencing machine that laid the groundwork for the human genome project*

DYSLEXIA IS A MIXTURE OF ABILITIES AND DIFFICULTIES. Because difficulties need supporting, this book has mainly focused on dyslexics' weak areas. However, dyslexics have strengths, too! This chapter has a slightly different format, as we explore the creative ways that dyslexic children solve problems.

Case study: Kieran and the questions (part 1)

Kieran always asked questions. He asked so many questions that people usually told him to shut up.

When his class learned about the solar system in school, Kieran asked: 'Why are black holes black?' He asked: 'What's *inside* a black hole?'

His teacher didn't have any answers for him, so she told him off for being disruptive. But Kieran wasn't disruptive. His head was just full of questions.

Over dinner that evening, Kieran asked his mum another burning question: 'If we had a magnet big enough, could we change the seasons?'

His mum just sighed and told him to eat his carrots.

Case study: April and the world's greatest desk (part 1)

April could see a million things around her that would work better, if only they were designed differently. When she was supposed to be doing her homework, she mentally redesigned the objects on her desk instead.

If you changed the shape of that pencil sharpener, it would be so much better. If you shifted the balance on that wooden toy, it would be way more fun.

She even redesigned the desk itself. April could see pictures in her mind of her designs. It all seemed so obvious to her.

April's dad told her she should put her designs down on paper, so she set about coming up with her grandest design yet: the world's greatest desk.

Case study: Zach and the essay (part 1)

The only part of school that Zach liked was lunchtime, which he usually spent drawing cartoons for the school newspaper. In fact, Zach spent most of his time drawing – even when he was supposed to be doing schoolwork.

Zach knew he was smart and creative. His head was full of ideas, but whenever he tried to write them down, the results weren't pretty. That was why Zach was dreading the essay about Tutankhamun that he was due to hand in. He had plenty of ideas, but his writing always ended up in the waste paper basket.

Finally, in desperation, Zach decided to look at his essay from a new angle. Instead of writing, he created a stop-motion animation. It featured miniature versions of the pyramids in Egypt, and the animation showed tiny clay archaeologists visiting the tombs and discovering Tutankhamun.

The morning that Zach's essay was due, he plonked down a USB stick on the desk of Mr Darby, his teacher. Mr Darby didn't look happy.

SIGNS OF DYSLEXIA

Asking questions no one else is asking

Dyslexic children tend to look at problems differently from other children. Like Kieran, they don't tend to ask the obvious questions or come up with the obvious solutions.

This is because a dyslexic brain files information in a different way from a non-dyslexic brain. Someone without dyslexia might mentally file the word 'pigeon' next to the word 'bird', because it's a type of bird. It's a filing system that any librarian would understand.

However, a dyslexic might file the word 'pigeon' next to the word 'school', because he sees a funny pigeon on the way to school every day. Dyslexic filing systems are highly personal. They might seem odd to other people, but, to the dyslexic child, they make perfect sense.

Making new connections

As a result of the dyslexic child's unconventional filing system, information takes a longer route as it travels through his brain. This is why dyslexic children struggle with rapid naming (coming up with the word they want in a hurry). Yet 'taking the long way' can also be a blessing.

Imagine the brain as a big, old house, filled with secret staircases and hidden passageways. A non-dyslexic who's trying to solve a problem would just walk straight through the house, using the shortest route possible. But a dyslexic child would go up and down different staircases, ducking into hidden passages. Each time he does so – *ping!* – he makes a new connection. Each new connection gives him a new idea for how to solve the problem.

Big-picture thinking

A dyslexic child's brain may make so many new connections that some of them are bound to be a bit bonkers. But others will be jaw-droppingly amazing. It's this kind of 'thinking outside the box' that can lead to a career as a business tycoon or a real-life action hero.

Did you know that the inspiration for the hero of *Jurassic Park* was a dyslexic palaeontologist? The character of Alan Grant was based on dinosaur expert Jack Horner, who credits some of his biggest scientific breakthroughs to his dyslexic ability to look beyond pre-conceived ideas.

Because of the way their brains process information, dyslexics tend to be 'big-picture thinkers'. They're not bothered by limitations. They don't sweat the small stuff. Their brains are going on new journeys every second.

Finding work-arounds in the classroom

These problem-solving smarts can serve dyslexic children well in later life, but most will also use them in the classroom. Many children come up with impressive 'work-arounds' to offset their own dyslexic weaknesses.

Let's consider a maths problem like **7 x 2**. This is a straightforward sum that might seem simple to a non-dyslexic child, but it's one that can be difficult for a dyslexic child to master, if his learning hasn't been supported properly. So he'll use a creative work-around instead. Using his creative method, it might take him longer to solve the problem, and he will usually work much harder than his classmates. This is because dyslexic work-arounds tend to be very complicated.

Work-arounds show a dyslexic child's creativity. But they can also be a reason his dyslexia stays hidden. Most children will be relieved to learn the 'easy' way to solve maths and English problems. This frees up a dyslexic child's mind to use his creativity elsewhere. He might start coming up with incredible inventions or amazing designs ...

3D design in your mind

For some dyslexics – but only some – their problem-solving ability goes beyond making unconventional connections. Children like April can also use their minds as 3D computer design programs. This subset of dyslexia involves superior visuo-spatial processing. This is the ability to manipulate objects mentally in 3D space.

Say a child wanted to design a robot. Even if he thought really hard about it, a regular child would probably only see a flat 2D image in his mind. It might be fuzzy around the edges and he wouldn't quite know how every part of the robot could work in real life.

A dyslexic child with superior visuo-spatial abilities, however, would be able to fully design the robot using just his mind. He could close his eyes and step inside his mental sketch of the robot. He could walk around the robot, twiddle every knob, press every button. It would feel as real as if the robot was right in front of him. Pretty amazing, huh? There's even a rumour that NASA employs a lot of dyslexics for exactly this reason!

Thinking in pictures

It's not surprising, then, that dyslexics with great visuo-spatial abilities often become designers, inventors or engineers. What do the Millennium Dome, Tommy Hilfiger clothes, and a set of photographs hanging in the National Portrait Gallery have in common?

Answer: they're all creations that come from dyslexic minds. Architect Richard Rogers, who designed the Millennium Dome, fashion designers Tommy Hilfiger and Paul Smith, and photographer David Bailey are all famously dyslexic. They're joined by an impressive set of dyslexic inventors and scientists, including William Dreyer and Nobel laureate, Carol Greider.

So ... do dyslexics make better artists and scientists because of innate strengths, or because they find reading and writing so difficult? It depends on the dyslexic, but it's likely to be a bit of both.

Even for children who don't want to be the next great designer or inventor, visuo-spatial skills can mean a new way to look at the world. Once a child learns to harness this 'mental computer program', he may find it easier to solve problems by creating pictures in his mind, rather than thinking about the problem in terms of words.

At the other end of the spectrum

Visuo-spatial ability is often considered the 'superpower' of dyslexia. It can be frustrating to learn, then, that not all dyslexics have this amazing visuo-spatial power. Some dyslexics have normal spatial-thought abilities. Other dyslexics actually have difficulties with spatial thought – particularly dyslexic-dyspraxic children, who may have poor spatial awareness.

Yet, even if your child does not have special visuo-spatial abilities, he still has an ace up his sleeve. Hard work and self-belief are the true ways to get ahead in life. And dyslexics may have an advantage there, as well ...

As outlined in *Chapter 7: Writing*, despite their difficulties with words, many dyslexics become authors. A natural interest in a subject (and lots of parental support!) can allow a child to turn a dyslexic weakness into a strength. Because their road to success may be harder, dyslexic children often develop better self-awareness and self-belief than other children.

Try, try, and try again!

A dyslexic child might have been told by teachers that he's stupid. He might have worked twice as hard as his classmates to get the same grade. He's likely to have faced failure, picked himself up, and tried again.

The great thing is: as long as you have the right mindset, adversity can be turned into a positive. Always being told you can't do something can make you stronger. It can make you determined to prove the naysayers wrong. It can make you say: *yes, actually, I can do that!*

In fact, a study by Cass Business School found that 19% of entrepreneurs in the UK are dyslexic. The number is even higher in the US, where 35% of entrepreneurs show signs of dyslexia. Richard Branson is just one dyslexic with a flair for business. He didn't learn to read until he was eight years old, and he left school with few qualifications. However, that didn't stop him from starting his own successful business (a magazine called *Student*) when he was a teenager. He's now a billionaire and one of the most successful businessmen ever. He credits his dyslexia with helping him to be 'more intuitive'.

After all, a lot of what it takes to succeed in life isn't natural ability or skill – it's confidence. Bounce-back-ability, if you will. If he tries to start a business or write a novel or, yes, design a robot, a non-dyslexic child might stop when it gets a bit hard. But a dyslexic child is much more likely to keep trying.

PROBLEM SOLVING – KEY SIGNS OF DYSLEXIA:

- Child asks unusual questions
- Comes up with outside-the-box solutions
- Makes up his own work-arounds
- May display amazing design ability

Case study: Kieran and the questions (part 2)

When Kieran had to write a sci-fi story for school, he came up with loads of ideas. He read out his story in class and everyone *oooh*'ed about the hero who had a magnet that could change the seasons.

When it was time for him to write a report on the solar system, Kieran begged his mum to take him to the science museum. He spent ages talking to the museum staff about black holes. He was so keen to know the answers to his questions that he learned more than anyone else in his class about the solar system. He got a gold star on his report.

Kieran's mum still can't help getting irritated at Kieran sometimes, but she knows that his questions are what make him exceptional.

Case study: April and the world's greatest desk (part 2)

April designed a desk that fitted perfectly into the funny-shaped corner of her bedroom. She designed three levels of storage, so that there was a cubby for everything she needed. She even put in a secret compartment.

April's dad was so impressed with her design that he set about making the desk. He spent weeks hammering and sawing, until April's design became a reality.

'You're amazing!' April told her dad, as she gazed at the world's greatest desk – her daydream come true.

Her dad shrugged and said, 'I just made it. You're the one who came up with the idea. That's the hard part.'

Case study: Zach and the essay (part 2)

When his teacher made him stay after school, Zach was sure he was in trouble.

'I watched your animation,' Mr Darby said.

Zach winced, waiting for Mr Darby to start shouting.

'I thought it was excellent,' Mr Darby said. 'I can see you put a lot of effort into it. And it shows you really paid attention to what we learned about Tutankhamun. So I'm giving you an A.'

Zach was stunned. 'Really?'

Mr Darby laughed. 'It doesn't mean you can do this every time. Next essay, I want words from you. But I appreciate your ingenuity.'

Zach didn't bother to ask what *ingenuity* meant. He was too overwhelmed with pride.

Later, Mr Darby had a chat with Zach's parents. He suggested that Zach should be assessed for dyslexia. When the assessment turned out to be positive, Zach's parents found a tutor for Zach. The tutor helped him to improve his writing.

Zach still prefers art, but he's starting to like writing more. Because he can write better now, he has started sending letters to newspapers and magazines. He's hoping one of them will publish his cartoons.

And, as he boasts in his letters, he once got an A on a school project, using stop-motion animation ...

15.

Co-occurring Conditions

> 66 99
>
> 'The really social people did not invent the first stone spear. It was probably invented by an Aspie who chipped away at rocks while the other people socialised around the campfire. Without autism traits, we might still be living in caves.'
>
> — **TEMPLE GRANDIN (autistic scientist)**
>
> *Professor of animal science and one of* Time *magazine's '100 Most Influential People'*

YOU WON'T ALWAYS FIND DYSLEXIA IN ITS 'PURE' FORM. Instead, a child may have a mish-mash of traits from dyslexia and one or two other learning difficulties. Working out the missing piece of the puzzle can make a big difference in understanding and supporting your child.

Dyslexia + _____? = Your Child's Learning Difficulties

AUTISM SPECTRUM DISORDER (ASD)

Dyslexia and Autism Spectrum Disorder (ASD), which both run in families, can often overlap. The good news is: autism traits can be used to offset dyslexic weaknesses, as long as the dyslexic-ASD child is supported in the right way.

Parents may be more familiar with the terms 'autism' or 'Asperger's Syndrome' (the high-functioning form of autism). However, experts now believe that it's better to talk about autism traits in terms of a spectrum that affects different children in different ways. So-called 'classic autism' describes children who have obvious problems with speech and movement. But many more children have mild autism traits that may not be so obvious.

Seeing the world in black and white

A child with ASD is likely to see the world in black and white terms, taking everything at face value. She may struggle to see things from someone else's perspective, so she won't understand how the people around her are feeling, or why they act the way they do.

She may also come across as very blunt. A child with ASD may take everything literally, which means idioms like 'it's raining cats and dogs' can make her feel confused or irritated. (There aren't *really* cats and dogs falling from the sky!)

A key sign of ASD is lack of eye contact during a conversation (although many children learn to compensate for this). A child with ASD won't get a lot of information from someone's facial expression, so she won't bother to look people in the eye.

What's more, a child with ASD is likely to struggle with social situations, because she can't grasp (or doesn't see any point to) polite chit-chat. Instead of having a 'typical' conversation, she may just begin talking at length about what *she* wants to talk about – usually her obsessions.

Special interests

Obsessions or special interests provide a way for children with ASD to relax. All children have particular interests, but an ASD obsession is likely to be all-consuming. If her special interest is lorries, a child with ASD might constantly recite facts about lorries. Her room might be filled to bursting with toy lorries. She might drag her parents out to the roadside every evening to go lorry-spotting.

Parents of ASD children are often amazed at how much their child can achieve as a result of her obsessions. Unprompted, she might learn a completely new language, or take apart a computer and figure out how it works! This is because children with ASD often have very good long-term memories, strong attention to detail, and the ability to concentrate for long periods of time.

Dealing with emotion differently

However, children with ASD often retreat into their obsessions, because they deal with emotion differently. Many children with ASD do not cry often, if at all. This simply isn't an emotional release for them. Instead, they are likely to have emotional 'meltdowns'.

A child with ASD who is dealing with lots of emotion may begin 'stimming'. This is short for 'self-stimulatory behaviour'. Flapping may be the most well-known type of stimming, but a child with ASD might also rock, spin, or repeat words over and over.

Overlap with dyspraxia

ASD has many similarities with dyspraxia. A child with ASD, like a child with dyspraxia, might have trouble getting her brain and her body to communicate. As a result, she might be clumsy and walk strangely.

A child with ASD might be hyper-sensitive to certain sensations, like sound or touch. A loud noise, like a dog barking, can feel unbearable for her. She may not like the sensation of being hugged or the feel of certain clothes on her skin. A child with ASD can also be *under*-sensitive to sensations, unable to judge hot or cold weather.

Mistaking dyslexia for ASD (and vice versa)

Parents should also bear in mind that dyslexia and ASD can look the same in certain situations. Dyslexic children can develop an odd speaking style that can come across like ASD. When asked a question in class, a dyslexic child might start talking at length about something that has nothing to do with the lesson.

This kind of verbal diarrhoea shouldn't be mistaken for ASD, however. If a child has ASD, she may talk at length about her obsessions and find it difficult to grasp the other person's non-verbal reactions. By contrast, a dyslexic child's monologues won't be on a particular, cherished subject. It's just that she has trouble ordering her thoughts, because of her weak working memory. A dyslexic child is likely to be embarrassed when the other person stops her, because she didn't mean to talk for so long. A child with ASD, on the other hand, probably won't realise she did anything out of the ordinary.

ASD in every walk of life

The word 'autism' can be understandably scary for parents. Yet the reality is simply a child who thinks a little differently ... which can be a very good thing! You'll find successful people with ASD in every walk of life: science, economics, music, acting, and more. Hollywood star Daryl

Hannah (*Splash*, *Kill Bill*), singer Gary Numan, and rapper Example all have ASD. In the academic world, Pulitzer-Prize-winning music critic Tim Page and Nobel-Prize-winning economist Vernon L. Smith both have ASD. Scientist Temple Grandin is both a professor of animal science and a best-selling author – and she credits autism with much of her success.

Key Signs of ASD:

- Child doesn't naturally make eye contact
- Very literal – doesn't understand figures of speech
- Extremely passionate about certain subjects
- Flaps, rocks or repeats words when upset

Case study: Tim and the pirates (part 1)

When Tim found a pirate hat in a charity shop, he used all of his pocket money to buy it. Tim loved pirates and he loved his pirate hat. He wore the pirate hat every single day, because it made him feel good. Tim's mum teased him, saying that he was the world's greatest expert on pirates. If anyone asked – and even if they didn't – he told them all about Blackbeard and Calico Jack and all the other famous pirates throughout history.

Tim knew so much about pirates that, one day, his mum suggested he write a book. Tim was excited about the idea; he was sure the book would be amazing. But, somehow, when he sat down to begin, it was a struggle to write even one sentence. Finally, he gave up in frustration.

SUPPORTING ASD

Visit a Clinical Psychologist for a formal ASD assessment. You should be able to get a referral from your GP. Educational Psychologists don't diagnose ASD, but they can give parents recommendations for action in school.

Match ASD strengths with dyslexic weaknesses. A child with ASD typically has strong attention to detail, good long-term memory, and the ability to concentrate for long periods of time. Parents can encourage their dyslexic-ASD child to use these strengths to do the repetition and over-learning that's necessary to master tricky skills like times tables and spelling rules.

Use ASD obsessions to make learning interesting. Simply put: if, like Tim, your child loves pirates, use pirates in every learning exercise. Maths problems about pirates! Handwriting practice about pirates! Writing stories about pirates! (For many ASD children, learning itself can become an obsession, if encouraged.)

Indulge ASD passions. Parents often despair that their ASD child doesn't do 'normal' things. This is natural, but instead of focusing on what your child doesn't do, support her in what she *does* do. Autism traits often include an obsessive need to understand how things work and a passionate interest in an unusual subject. These traits can be positive and lead to an exciting career, as long as the child is supported along the way.

Build self-esteem by encouraging your child to get involved with activities where she can meet children with similar interests. A child with ASD is particularly at risk of becoming socially isolated, so extra opportunities to make friends are important.

Rehearse how to act in social situations. While other children naturally pick up social cues, a child with ASD may need to actively learn 'soft skills', like how to make small talk and how to play with other children. Role-playing these situations with your child, using stories, or creating comic strips, complete with dialogue bubbles, can help her to become more confident.

Counselling or coaching from a professional can also help a child with ASD to relate better to those around her.

Case study: Tim and the pirates (part 2)

Tim had been diagnosed with Autism Spectrum Disorder when he was young, and his parents assumed that any problems he had in school were a result of ASD. They always stressed the positives of his ASD (his inquiring mind and his off-beat obsessions were what made Tim *Tim*), but they were worried that he was falling behind in school.

When one of Tim's teachers suggested that he might also be dyslexic, everything fell into place. Tim's parents found out how they could support Tim's dyslexia. They were able to use his pirate obsession to coax Tim into practising writing, spelling and other things he found difficult. Tim's mum created lots of pirate-themed worksheets, which Tim would happily sit and do for hours. She also encouraged him to practise his handwriting by copying out passages from his favourite pirate books.

Tim's writing has improved so much that he has started work on his own pirate book again. It's slow going, but his mum and dad are helping him. He's determined to finish the book and prove that he really is the world's greatest expert on pirates!

ATTENTION DEFICIT (AND HYPERACTIVITY) DISORDER (ADD/ADHD)

A child with dyslexia is more likely to have Attention Deficit (and Hyperactivity) Disorder (ADD/ADHD) than a non-dyslexic child. Like dyslexia, ADHD runs in families. It may even have a similar genetic basis to dyslexia.

A child with ADHD is impulsive, restless, and easily distracted. Despite the name, it's not that an attention-deficit child can't pay attention. It's just that she can't always pay attention to the right things.

Paying attention to the wrong things

A child with ADHD can't easily control the amount of attention she gives to passing thoughts or things happening around her. A non-ADHD child might ignore the sound of a dog barking while she's doing her homework. But a child with ADHD is more likely to go outside and see if she can find the dog, or begin daydreaming about how much she wants a dog.

If your child has ADHD, it means she can't filter out distractions easily. She *is* able to concentrate. In fact, she may 'hyperfocus', devoting a massive amount of attention to one thing. But she may find it hard to concentrate on the task at hand.

Looking for the next exciting thing

A child with ADHD isn't good at waiting. She needs attention or positive reinforcement – right now! As a result, she's likely to be very impulsive. She's always looking for something new, exciting, or stimulating.

If there's a brightly-coloured or tactile object nearby, she'll pick it up – even if she's not supposed to. The search for the next exciting thing can leave an ADHD child suffering from mood swings: up one minute, down the next.

She may also say things without thinking. What she says could be mean or just meaningless. She simply can't control the impulse to speak. Her impulsivity may also lead her to steal, break things, or even hit people.

With or without hyperactivity

A child with ADHD may be always bouncing off the walls – or she may just sit and daydream. The common term is Attention Deficit and Hyperactivity Disorder, but the disorder can present with or without hyperactivity.

If your child can't sit still, even for a few minutes, it's likely that she's hyperactive. This can make it easier to spot ADHD. However, parents should be aware that a child can be hyperactive without having ADHD. Food allergies, including bad reactions to artificial additives (the kind found in fizzy drinks and sweets, for example), can also cause hyperactivity.

What's more, a child who is attention-deficit, but not hyperactive, may be harder to diagnose. These children can go through life labelled as daydreamers or 'just lazy', because their type of Attention Deficit Disorder causes them to drift off and give passing thoughts too much attention.

Mistaking dyslexia for ADHD (and vice versa)

ADHD and dyslexia are often mixed up, because a child with ADHD and a child with dyslexia may appear the same to the untrained eye. For both children, their progress at school is likely to be slow. They'll be working at a lower level than they should be. They're also likely to have low self-esteem, having been told they're 'stupid', 'lazy', or a 'trouble-maker'.

A child with ADHD and a child with dyslexia may even *act* the same way sometimes. Both are likely to call out in class or make interruptions – but for different reasons. Poor impulse control in children with ADHD means that they may shout out an answer or make constant interruptions. A dyslexic child might make the same kind of interruptions, but it's not impulse control that's the problem. It's weak working memory, which means that she can't keep a thought in her head without voicing it. A dyslexic-dyspraxic child with poor balance may also be movement-seeking, but it's simply that she is adjusting her body to try and get comfortable, rather than showing signs of hyperactivity.

Also remember that low self-esteem may make it seem like a dyslexic child is very easily distracted. Her anxiety about learning might make her fidgety and desperate to do anything except homework. That's not ADHD – it's fear. Some children, like Lucy (see case study), are wrongly diagnosed with ADHD, when it's actually dyslexia that's the root of their struggles. Many more children, of course, may have a combination of dyslexia and ADHD, so their learning must be supported in a way that's both dyslexia-friendly *and* ADHD-friendly.

Understanding and supporting ADHD

ADHD is perhaps even less well understood than dyslexia. Don't buy the media hype that parents of ADHD children are just overreacting or choosing to medicate problem children. This is not true – and it's also not true that children with ADHD won't make anything of their lives.

Many athletes with ADHD have channelled their excess energy into sporting greatness. Michael Phelps, an Olympic swimmer, Greg LeMond, a three-time winner of the Tour de France, and Louis Smith, an Olympic gymnast, have all been diagnosed with ADHD.

You'll also find the (famous) face of ADHD on the stage and screen: Britney Spears, Justin Timberlake, Zooey Deschanel, and Will Smith all have ADHD. (In fact, Will Smith has both ADHD and dyslexia.) Comedian Rory Bremner even credits his ADHD with allowing him to 'think laterally in the comedic sense'. This proves that, as long as ADHD is supported in the right way, it can be a positive, not a negative.

KEY SIGNS OF ADHD:

- Child is easily distracted
- Attention-seeking
- Impulsive

Case study: Caleb, the funny one (part 1)

Caleb was the funny one in school. He often got out of his seat and made faces behind the teacher's back. He shouted out rude things in class, which made everyone laugh.

Everyone agreed that Caleb was funny, but no one wanted to sit next to him.

At home, all of his toys were missing arms and legs, because Caleb couldn't resist pulling the toys apart. He stole chocolate bars out of the kitchen cupboards. And he often lied about how much homework he'd done.

Even when his mum stood over him while he did his homework, he couldn't concentrate on anything for more than a few minutes. His dad tried to get him to practise the things that he was bad at, like times tables and spelling, but he refused. He'd struggled for so long that he wouldn't even try anymore.

He pretended he didn't care and cracked a joke instead. Sometimes, however, Caleb wished he wasn't just 'the funny one'.

Case study: Lucy, who couldn't finish (part 1)

Lucy could never quite finish anything. She handed in her homework half-finished – or simply didn't hand it in at all. She ran out of time in exams. Even when she was called on in class, she wasn't quick enough to come up with an answer. Sometimes she even trailed off in the middle of a ...

Finally, one of Lucy's teachers suggested the problem might be Attention Deficit Disorder. Lucy got a diagnosis for ADD and she was prescribed medication.

Yet Lucy still struggled in school. Her progress was still achingly slow, even though she was clearly bright. Her mind still wandered when she tried to do her homework. Her doctor increased her ADD medication. Then he changed it to a different type of medication. Still there was no change for Lucy.

SUPPORTING *ADHD*

Visit a Clinical Psychologist for a formal ADHD assessment. You'll normally be able to get a referral through your GP. Educational Psychologists don't diagnose ADHD, but they can give parents recommendations for action in school.

Medication can help a child with ADHD to focus more easily. Different types of ADHD need different medication. Stimulants or anti-depressants (or a combination) may be prescribed. For an ADHD child, this medication doesn't actually work as a stimulant or an anti-depressant – it just helps her to fight the distractibility, impulsivity and restlessness of ADHD.

Counselling or coaching from a professional can also help a child with ADHD to control her impulses and focus better.

Rule out food allergies as a cause of hyperactivity by visiting your GP for a patch test, seeing a nutritionist, keeping a food diary, or doing an elimination diet.

Give lots of praise. A child with ADHD and dyslexia is doubly prone to low self-esteem, so make sure to praise even small achievements. Getting your child involved in non-school activities (like sports, choir, or local theatre) can also allow her to build self-esteem.

Structure and security are important for a child with ADHD. This means putting in place a set of rules – rules that always stay the same. If your child acts badly on impulse, she needs tough love.

Treat every day as a fresh start. Don't dwell on things that your ADHD child did wrong yesterday. Make it clear that today's a new chance to make good choices.

Change the learning environment, so that your child doesn't have as much to be distracted by while she's doing homework. Get rid of brightly-coloured, tactile objects; shut pets in another room; ban background music and TV.

Case study: Caleb, the funny one (part 2)

One of Caleb's teachers suggested that he might have ADHD, so his parents took him to see a Clinical Psychologist for an assessment. Caleb was amazed to find out there was a reason his brain worked this way – and there were other people like him in the world.

Caleb's parents began taking him to regular counselling sessions with an ADHD expert, and they put in place a firm set of rules for Caleb to follow at home. Slowly, Caleb's behaviour began to improve.

What's more, Caleb found a new hobby. He started recording video blogs on his computer. He could talk about his experiences and share them with the whole Internet. And people actually responded! Through his videos, he found lots of other kids with ADHD, who understood what he was going through.

Best of all, the video blogs were a great way for him to practise his stand-up comedy material. After finding out that Rory Bremner has ADHD, Caleb decided he wanted to become a real comedian. He wanted to make people laugh for the right reasons.

Case study: Lucy, who couldn't finish (part 2)

Lucy was confused by what the Educational Psychologist said. If the other doctor had told her she did have ADD, how could it be that she *didn't* have ADD?

'It's not a trick or a scam,' Mrs Wesley, the Educational Psychologist, told Lucy. 'It's just a mistake. When the difference is inside the brain, it can be hard to tell exactly what the root cause is.'

Lucy was still confused, but she supposed these things happened.

After Mrs Wesley diagnosed Lucy with dyslexia, Lucy stopped taking her ADD medication and started seeing a dyslexia tutor instead. Secretly, Lucy wondered if this new diagnosis wasn't just another mistake. The other 'fix' hadn't worked – why would this one?

Yet Lucy began to look forward to her weekly tutoring sessions. It wasn't a *quick* fix, but Lucy began to find her schoolwork slightly easier. She was able to finish her homework assignments for the first time ever. And, with extra time allowed, as a result of her dyslexia diagnosis, she was able to finish her exam papers. Slowly but surely, Lucy built up her skills, and her confidence grew and grew.

Now, when the teacher calls on Lucy in class, she has the confidence to stop, think for a moment, and say the answer – without trailing off in the middle of a sentence.

16.

GETTING A DIAGNOSIS

IF YOU THINK YOUR CHILD IS DYSLEXIC, THERE ARE SEVERAL different paths available to you. There's no right or wrong way forward. Just as every child is different, every parent will have different views on getting a formal diagnosis.

Next, I'll help you to weigh the pros and cons of each option, learn what to expect from a standard assessment, and find out what arrangements your child is entitled to in school.

> **Note:**
> This chapter is specific to state schools and procedures in the UK, although the general advice may be helpful to those outside of the UK.

'SHOULD I GET A FORMAL DIAGNOSIS?'

Depending on your child's age and needs, parents may decide to get a diagnosis through the school, get a private assessment, or forgo formal assessment altogether. There are five main options available to you:

Option 1: Don't get a formal diagnosis

Pros:

- Free
- No paperwork
- No tests
- Child won't be 'labelled'

Cons:

- No classroom provisions in school
- No special allowances in exams
- No list of recommendations from a professional
- Child may feel he's 'the only one'

If you feel able to support your dyslexic child's learning at home, there's no reason you have to get a formal diagnosis. A diagnosis doesn't actually *do* anything. If a child is already doing well in school, and particularly if he's older, there might not be much to gain from a diagnosis. However, parents must be ready to take charge of their child's learning, since he will need special support to realise his full potential.

Advice:

- Talk to your child's teacher about his dyslexia, so that he receives support in school.
- Explain to the child what dyslexia is, so that he doesn't feel alone.
- Read widely, so that you can answer questions when they arise.
- Weekly tutoring sessions with a dyslexia expert can help to keep your child on track.

Option 2: Get a diagnosis via the school

Pros:

- Free
- Parents and child have a sense of certainty
- Classroom provisions in school
- Special allowances in exams
- School has a legal obligation to deliver support

Cons:

- Very long process
- Lots of paperwork

- Child has to undergo lots of tests
- Parents have no choice, in terms of the assessment or the assessor

If your child shows signs of dyslexia, his school will be able to refer him to a Chartered Psychologist (usually an Educational Psychologist) or a Specialist Assessor for a diagnosis. This process is free for parents – but it takes a long time. There are lots of children with dyslexia and not much public money to diagnose them.

The school may seek advice from other professionals before contacting the Educational Psychologist/Specialist Assessor. Sometimes, a non-specialist teacher will administer a screener (see option 5) and discount dyslexia on the basis of these limited results. Other times, a professional may draw conclusions after only observing a child in class or looking over his work.

If your child is given an assessment that seems very short and doesn't include the tests mentioned in the second part of this chapter, it may be a sign that only a screening and planning assessment (option 5) has been carried out. In these cases, parents should push for a full dyslexia assessment, carried out by an Educational Psychologist or Specialist Assessor, which is what your child is entitled to.

However, the bottom line is: the school is in control of the process, since they are paying. The school also controls the timescale. This can be frustrating for parents, since children can wait up to a year for a diagnosis.

If the child is young, it might not matter if he has to wait a year. Parents can begin supporting his learning at home in the meantime. By the time he reaches senior school, he'll have his diagnosis and the allowances that come with it. He'll also be entitled to consideration for retesting, to obtain special exam arrangements (e.g. extra time in exams). However, parents of an older child, or one who is struggling a lot in school, may not want to wait such a long time for a diagnosis.

Parents should also bear in mind that getting their child's school to take action may be an uphill battle. Primary schools often prefer to spend their limited budget on supporting additional needs, rather than diagnosing them. Yet, conversely, secondary schools are less likely to test for dyslexia and may expect a diagnosis to be in place when the child starts Year 7.

For this reason, don't be afraid to be a pushy parent! Don't just talk to the class teacher. Also talk to the head teacher and SENCo (Special Educational Needs Coordinator) – repeatedly, if necessary. Gather examples of your child's work that prove he has specific issues that need supporting (e.g. weak spelling). Don't let yourself be fobbed off. Don't give up. Be prepared to push for action.

Advice:

- Be patient but diligent when talking to the school. Understand that it may be a long wait, but don't let your child slip through the cracks, either.
- Pay attention to the exact assessments being carried out and the qualifications of the assessor.
- Start supporting your child at home – speaking to a local dyslexia tutor or joining your local dyslexia association can help you to get started.

Option 3: Get a diagnosis from an Educational Psychologist

Pros:

- Quick to arrange
- Expert, tailored advice
- Parents and child have a sense of certainty
- Classroom provisions in school
- Special allowances in exams

Cons:

- Expensive
- Child has to undergo lots of tests

- Schools don't have to accept the recommendations/allowances
- Hard for parents and class teachers to understand the report
- Assessors may vary in how up-to-date their knowledge of dyslexia is

Going direct to an Educational Psychologist (EP) takes the hassle out of getting a diagnosis – but it also costs money.

Getting a quick diagnosis from an independent EP means that parents get expert, tailored advice on their child's dyslexia straight away. With this formal diagnosis, the child can get all the same allowances he'd get following a school EP's diagnosis – without waiting. Obviously, not every child will meet the criteria to be diagnosed with dyslexia, but parents should nonetheless get a tailored list of recommendations to help their child.

A word of warning: make sure that you have written assurances from the school that the recommendations from the assessment will be accepted. Parents should check beforehand that the school will accept their chosen assessor. Occasionally, schools will only accept a diagnosis from a 'known quantity'.

Although most EPs are very highly trained, parents should go into the process of finding an EP with their eyes open. It's worth getting recommendations from other parents or local dyslexia experts. Dyslexia knowledge quickly goes out of date and some EPs' assessments may not reflect the latest thinking on dyslexia. Pick a friendly and helpful EP, if possible. An EP's dyslexia report can be hard for laypeople to understand, so make sure he or she is happy to spend time explaining the report to you, and willing to answer additional questions over the phone at a later stage.

Advice:

- For a child with exams coming up, parents may consider it worth the cost to get a quick diagnosis.
- Ensure the school will accept the diagnosis/recommendations before going ahead with the paid assessment.
- Make sure the Educational Psychologist is happy to spend time explaining the specifics of the report.

Option 4: Get a diagnosis from a Specialist Assessor

Other professionals are also able to offer dyslexia screening and diagnosis. The term Specialist Assessor is generally used to describe teachers who hold Associate

Membership of the British Dyslexia Association (AMBDA) status, an advanced qualification in dyslexia diagnosis. This qualification means that, by law, they can carry out official diagnostic screenings, which enable the child to receive special allowances in school. You may also wish to find an assessor with an SpLD Assessment Practising Certificate (APC) from PATOSS (Professional Association of Teachers of Students with Specific Learning Difficulties).

The pros and cons of enlisting the services of a Specialist Assessor are much the same as for option 3. This kind of testing involves payment, but it can be done pronto, allowing the child to quickly receive an official diagnosis and support in school.

A Specialist Assessor may be independent, or work as part of a professional organisation or charity, but parents should always check that their AMBDA status is current. The tests carried out by a Specialist Assessor are different from those carried out by an Educational Psychologist, but the assessment will still be comprehensive. However, parents should check beforehand that the school will accept the diagnosis and recommendations from their chosen assessor.

Advice:

- Get recommendations from other parents and local dyslexia tutors.
- Make sure you'll receive a formal diagnosis.
- Check the qualifications of the assessor.
- Ensure the school will accept the diagnosis/recommendations.

Option 5: Get a screening and planning assessment

Pros:

- Quick to arrange
- Quick to carry out
- Lower cost than a formal assessment

Cons:

- Assessor may not be a qualified professional
- Schools don't have to accept the recommendations/allowances

Parents may also be offered a more limited dyslexia assessment, which simply screens for dyslexia, but does not provide an official diagnosis. The testing process tends to be shorter and, therefore, the cost will be lower. This type of screening can be used to identify weak areas, and makes it possible to form a plan of action for ongoing support and teaching. Because it's much less formal, the assessment can be tailored to a particular area of concern (e.g. if a child primarily struggles with maths, the assessment can focus on how the child deals with maths problems). Following the assessment, parents should receive a report on how to support their child's learning, which can be shared with teachers and tutors.

However, parents should be aware that these screenings are not usually carried out by professionals with advanced qualifications. And, because full testing is not included, the diagnosis will not be accepted by schools and exam boards. An informal screening of this type may be a good first step, but parents on a budget might prefer to put their money towards a full diagnosis from an Educational Psychologist or Specialist Assessor.

Advice:

- Get recommendations from other parents and local dyslexia tutors.
- Check the qualifications of the assessor.
- Make sure the report you'll receive will be genuinely helpful in supporting your child's learning.

'WHAT DOES A FORMAL DIAGNOSIS MEAN FOR MY CHILD?'

Getting a diagnosis can be a long and sometimes expensive process. However, once your child has a formal diagnosis (received from an Educational Psychologist or Specialist Assessor), parents can expect certain provisions to be put in place. It's important to make sure your child has everything to which he's entitled.

'Assess, Plan, Do, Review'

Once your child's dyslexia has been identified, and sometimes before the formal diagnosis has been made, the school will draw up an action plan for him. Formerly called an Individual Education Plan (IEP), this action plan is now given different names by different schools, but generally follows the framework of 'Assess, Plan, Do, Review'. It will typically list three or four short-term targets for the child's learning, focusing on the core areas of communication, literacy, maths, and behaviour. It should be reviewed, with the parents included in the review, at least twice a year.

This action plan provides structure for your child. It means that the parents, the child, and the school all know where they stand. However, it doesn't guarantee extra help for your child. This means that parents should stay on top of the school. Keep in regular contact with the class teacher, the head teacher, *and* the SENCo. Make sure your child really is working towards the targets on his plan and that those targets are SMART (Specific, Measurable, Attainable, Relevant, and Timely).

EHC plan

In rare cases, a dyslexic child might receive an EHC (Education, Health, and Care) plan, formerly called a Statement of Special Educational Needs. A child with an EHC plan may receive special equipment or one-to-one time with a teaching assistant. However, funding is now so limited that EHC plans are usually only given to children who are severely at risk and/or those who have complex, co-occurring difficulties.

At university

At university level, a dyslexic student can apply for the **Disabled Students' Allowance**. This is a grant, based on the family income, which can be used to buy special equipment, like dyslexia-friendly computer software.

Exam and classroom allowances

A formal dyslexia diagnosis also allows your child special provisions and allowances, both during exams and in the classroom. In fact, it is a good idea to establish practices like using a word processor or having a reader as the child's 'normal way of working' before formal exams. This way, he will be more likely to be granted the same allowances during his GCSEs and A-Levels.

Extra time

A dyslexic child is entitled to up to 25% extra time in exams. So, for a two-hour exam, your child might be allowed two-and-a-half hours. This is to compensate for dyslexics' slower processing speed and/or other difficulties.

How much extra time your child receives depends on his dyslexia assessment. A child who showed only slight problems with processing speed during the Educational Psychologist's tests might only be entitled to 10% extra time.

Use of a word processor

A dyslexic child may be allowed to use a computer word processing program (with spell checker disabled) to type his exams, instead of writing them by hand.

A child with dyspraxia traits may have very poor handwriting which can't be read by examiners, making a word processor necessary. If a dyslexic child simply finds working on a computer an easier way to order his thoughts (and avoid making lots of crossings-out on his exam paper), he may also be allowed to use a word processor.

It's not just in exams that use of a word processor may be allowed. He may be allowed to type instead of hand-write his homework/classwork, even if this isn't the usual practice for every student.

Use of a transcript

In some cases, a teacher or other adult may be allowed to make a transcript of a dyslexic student's exam paper. The adult will rewrite all of the child's answers in a clean answer booklet, which is then sent to the examiner, along with the child's original exam script. The examiner marks the original script, but can refer to the transcript for clarification.

This may be an option if the child's handwriting is illegible (due to dyspraxia), or if the child writes phonetically (due to dyslexia), making his writing very difficult to read.

Use of a scribe

A scribe is a person who writes down the child's answers during an exam. This means the child can concentrate on his answers without worrying about handwriting, spelling, or grammar. (However, as a result, the child won't normally get any marks for spelling and grammar.)

Scribes are generally only used if the child is dyspraxic and cannot use a word processor, or if his spelling and grammar are extremely poor, or if he writes so slowly that even extra time doesn't help him.

(A scribe is not allowed in Modern Foreign Language papers, unless the child can dictate foreign words letter by letter.)

Use of a reader or computer reader

A reader is a person who reads the questions on an exam paper to the child. A computer reader (a machine that reads out what's on the page) may be used instead. If a dyslexic child's diagnosis shows that he has very poor reading ability, he may be granted the use of a reader.

Use of coloured overlays

A dyslexic child will normally be allowed to use coloured overlays during exams, including reading rulers and virtual overlays.

'WHAT TESTS DOES THE ASSESSMENT INVOLVE?'

A full dyslexia assessment may take two or three hours. However, the assessor will do his or her best to put the child at ease. The assessment shouldn't be unpleasant, but it may be tiring. (In fact, the assessment will probably be more stressful for the parents than the child!)

A typical assessment will include some (though not all) of the following tests:

> **British Ability Scales, Third Edition (BAS3)**
> BAS3 tests cognitive skills, like perception and reasoning. There are 20 short tests in BAS3, testing verbal ability, non-verbal reasoning, and spatial ability. Your child may be asked to build a design using cubes or recreate a line drawing from memory.
>
> **Comprehensive Test of Phonological Processing, Second Edition (CTOPP-2)**
> CTOPP-2 tests how well a child can recognise and manipulate the sounds that make up words. There are several sub-tests of CTOPP-2, but a child might be tested on: elision (missing out one sound in a word); blending letters to make words; rapid naming; reversals of words; repeating nonsense words; or breaking up words into individual sounds.

Detailed Assessment of Speed of Handwriting (DASH)

DASH tests fine motor skills and how quickly and neatly a child can write. Children are tested on how quickly they can copy out a sentence two times: once in their 'best' handwriting; once in their 'fastest' handwriting. Children are also asked to do some free-writing (on a subject like 'my favourite teacher').

Gray Oral Reading Test, Fourth Edition (GORT-4)

GORT-4 tests a child's reading ability. The child is asked to read a passage aloud and he is scored on how quickly he reads and whether he pronounces each word correctly. After he has finished reading, he is asked questions on the content of the passage, in order to test his reading comprehension.

Neale Analysis of Reading Ability (NARA)

NARA tests a child's reading ability. The child is asked to read a series of written passages, which get harder as he reads on. The passages are designed to find out how fast and accurately the child can read and how well he understands what he reads.

Test of Auditory Processing Skills, Third Edition (TAPS-3)

TAPS-3 tests how well a child processes what he hears. To test auditory discrimination, the assessor speaks two words aloud and asks the child to say whether they are the same word or different. The child may also be tested on blending letters to make words; breaking up words into individual sounds; and on the strength of his short-term memory when it comes to words and sentences.

Test of Word Reading Efficiency, Second Edition (TOWRE-2)

TOWRE-2 tests a child's reading ability. The child is given a list of words. He is tested on how many of them he can read aloud in just 45 seconds. He is then given a list of nonsense words. Again, he is tested on how many of the nonsense words he can read aloud in 45 seconds.

Wechsler Individual Achievement Test, Second Edition (WIAT-II)

WIAT-II tests a child's academic progress: how well he has learned key skills from school. WIAT-II focuses on reading, maths, writing, and oral language. The tests will be familiar from school, involving reading comprehension or essay writing.

Wechsler Intelligence Scale for Children, Fourth Edition (WISC-IV)

WISC-IV tests a child's IQ. It's incredibly wide-ranging, testing everything from verbal comprehension to spotting the missing parts of a picture. The assessor may use all or just part of WISC-IV.

UNDERSTANDING THE ASSESSMENT RESULTS

Percentile score

Your child may be given a percentile score (e.g. 'he is on the 45th percentile'). This helps you to understand how well he compares to other children of the same age, in terms of reading ability (for example).

Imagine a group of 100 children, all of the same age. If your child scores on the 21st percentile, that means 21 of the children (including him) are the same or worse than him at reading; 79 of the children around him are better at reading. In simple terms: a low score is weak; a high score is strong.

Parents of dyslexic children will often find their child has a high percentile score in some areas (non-verbal reasoning, for example), but a low percentile score in areas like reading, spelling, or maths.

Age equivalent

Your child may be given an age equivalent – he has a 'reading age' of 8 or a 'maths age' of 12. This is the average age at which 50% of children would be reading at this level or doing maths at this level.

IQ

Your child's IQ may be tested. The average IQ is 100, with most of the population testing between 85 and 115.

WHEN A DIAGNOSIS IS WRONG

It's a parent's nightmare: 'I know my child is dyslexic, but in the assessment, he came out as non-dyslexic!'

Assessors vary in expertise, so it *can* happen. Educational Psychologists and Specialist Assessors are highly trained and will usually spot a child's dyslexia. However, they may choose to label it as a 'specific learning difficulty' or as 'dyslexic-type tendencies', especially if it's not a full or independent assessment.

During a full assessment, there are three major reasons why a dyslexic child might 'fail' a dyslexia diagnosis:

Being 'too good'

If a child is very bright, he may mask his dyslexia convincingly. Or, if he has received help at home or from a tutor, he may have learned to compensate for his dyslexia.

In the assessment, he'll ace tests that should reveal his dyslexia. This is not because he's *not* dyslexic. It's because he has so many strategies in place that he can pass the tests in spite of his dyslexia.

Advice:

- Make sure your child knows to be honest. He can tell the assessor if he's using a work-around on a test.
- If someone asks for an example of your child's work, give a real example, not one that's been worked on and re-drafted.
- If your child has a lot of strategies in place, bear in mind that a formal diagnosis might not even be necessary at this age. In some circumstances, it may be better to wait until your child begins to struggle.

'Dunno' syndrome

If a child has low self-esteem, he may not even try to answer questions during the assessment. He's so used to getting answers wrong because of his dyslexia that he'll just say, 'Dunno.'

Assessors used to hold that a child had to have an average or above-average IQ to be deemed dyslexic. This has now been revised, but the idea lingers for many assessors. Therefore, if a child appears to be of low intelligence, he might not be deemed dyslexic. His progress could be considered on a par with his IQ.

Advice:

- Explain to your child that dyslexia affects the brain's processing speed. It's okay to sit and think for a moment before answering a question.
- Encourage your child to be completely honest with the assessor about what he finds difficult and why.

Co-occurring conditions

Co-occurring conditions, such as Attention Deficit (and Hyperactivity) Disorder (ADHD) and Autism Spectrum Disorder (ASD), can also affect straightforward diagnosis. Specialist Assessors are trained to spot only dyslexia, while Educational Psychologists, despite their broader training, do not diagnose ADHD or ASD.

Parents must be aware that a child with multiple co-occurring conditions may be misdiagnosed with just one condition (ADHD, for example, when the true diagnosis should be ADHD with dyslexia). Alternatively, a co-occurring condition can end up masking the child's dyslexia (which is what can happen with over-achieving autistic-dyslexic children).

Advice:

- Even if your child doesn't have a formal diagnosis for a co-occurring condition, it's still worth flagging up your concerns to the assessor, if you believe he has ASD or ADHD traits that may skew the diagnosis results.

- Also speak to the assessor about the type of tests used for the dyslexia screening. Standardised tests for dyslexia don't always meet the needs of children with ADHD or ASD, and some assessments (e.g. BAS3 and CTOPP-2) can be more helpful than others. Consider 'shopping around' to find an assessor who properly meets your child's needs.

Following an assessment, if you feel your child's dyslexia has been dismissed in error, it may be worth getting a second opinion on the screening scores, or finding another professional to run a different set of tests.

17.

GETTING ADDITIONAL HELP

GETTING A DIAGNOSIS FOR A DYSLEXIC CHILD IS JUST THE beginning. Following the diagnosis, parents will usually want to find expert help, to make sure their child gets the right support. This could mean paying for private schooling or tutoring, or finding group dyslexia sessions. There are pros and cons to each option, so I'll help you to figure out what's right for your child.

> **Note:**
> This chapter is specific to state schools and procedures in the UK, although the general advice may be helpful to those outside of the UK.

Specialist dyslexia schools

Pros:

- Teachers educated about dyslexia
- Supportive environment
- Learning tailored to dyslexic children
- All the latest technology
- Small class sizes

Cons:

- Expensive
- Unregulated – quality may vary between schools
- Daily travel or boarding might be necessary
- Child may not get a well-rounded education

There are a handful of specialist independent schools in the UK, designed just for dyslexic children. The teachers tend to be highly trained in supporting dyslexia. Pupils will also be able to have sessions with speech therapists, occupational therapists, and other specialists, as needed.

Because everything's geared towards dyslexics, children will usually have access to technology that helps them to learn, such as text-to-speech software and Dictaphones to record lessons. Being surrounded by other dyslexics can also boost a child's self-esteem and help her to realise she's not 'the only one'.

The downside is that specialist schools come with a hefty price tag – and they're unregulated, so parents can't always be sure they're getting their money's worth. Unless the school is nearby, the child may have to board, or travel a long way to school each day.

What's more, the curriculum at specialist schools may be very focused on improving the pupils' English and maths. Therefore, children may not spend as much time on other subjects, like science, history, or art.

Advice:

- Specialist schools are right for some children, but not for others.
- Talk to existing parents of children at specialist schools.
- Ask an expert (such as an Educational Psychologist or a dyslexia tutor) for his or her opinion.

Note:

There are a very small number of specialist dyslexia schools in the UK that are state-funded and therefore free. As you would expect, these schools are very popular and hard to get into.

Private schools

Pros:

- Small class sizes
- Good facilities
- High academic standards

Cons:

- Expensive
- Unregulated – quality may vary between schools
- Teachers without teaching qualifications
- High academic standards can make it hard for dyslexic children to keep up

Private schooling can seem like a good option if there isn't a specialist dyslexia school in your area. However, many private schools are very results-driven. School days are long, there's lots of homework, and pupils are often expected to be working at a high academic level.

In light of this, many private schools have an entrance exam, which a dyslexic child may struggle to pass. (See the section on grammar schools, for more on why dyslexic children find entrance exams difficult.) What's more, a less-able student at a private school may be seen as dragging down the results.

Not all private schools are results-driven, however. A

dyslexic child may do well at a less rigorous private school, due to the small class sizes and high levels of teacher attention. There are some private schools that have a focus on Special Educational Needs. Often, these are 'preparatory' schools for younger children, designed to improve their basic skills, so that they can do well at senior-school level.

However, teaching quality may vary at private schools, where a teaching qualification isn't required. And some private schools have little or no provisions for dyslexic children.

Advice:

- For younger children, 'preparatory' private school can provide good basic skills (although a good state primary may do just as well).
- However, a results-driven private school is likely to make a dyslexic child feel stressed out and inadequate.

Grammar schools

Pros:

- Free
- High academic standards

Cons:

- High academic standards can make it hard for dyslexic children to keep up
- Dyslexic children will often struggle to pass the 11-plus exam
- Little support for special needs

For parents who can't afford private schooling for their child, grammar school can seem like the next best thing. However, like results-driven private schools, grammar schools tend to be very academic, so a child with dyslexic weaknesses is likely to struggle.

Many grammar schools don't put money into supporting special needs or investing in the types of technology (text-to-speech software, Dictaphones, etc.) that can help dyslexic learners – although this is in the process of changing. Be aware, as well, that a dyslexic child's self-esteem may be damaged by being around children who learn much more easily than she does, as tends to be the case in competitive grammar schools.

Dyslexic children may also find it particularly difficult to pass the 11-plus exam. This exam deliberately puts children under time pressure. We already know that a dyslexic child needs extra time in exams, because of her weak working memory and slow processing speed. Yet she is unlikely to be given extra time during the 11-plus (at least, not without lots of form-filling and jumping through hoops). Many 11-plus questions also depend on the child having a strong grasp of sequences, number facts, proofreading, and reading comprehension – all of which are common dyslexic weaknesses.

Advice:

- Grammar school may make a dyslexic child feel stressed out and inadequate.

State schools

Pros:

- Free
- Highly regulated
- Broad curriculum
- By law, special needs must be monitored

Cons:

- Real support for special needs will vary
- Large class sizes and 'streaming' may mean a dyslexic child doesn't reach her full potential

Although state schools may be the default option, for many dyslexic children they can be a positive experience. At senior-school level, children will be educated in a wide range of subjects, taught by subject specialists. Since many dyslexic children struggle with English and maths, but excel at other subjects, like science or art, this can boost their self-esteem.

State schools are also required to provide help for special needs. A SENCo (Special Educational Needs Coordinator) or Learning Support Coordinator should be on hand to make sure all the teachers are aware of a child's dyslexia.

As many parents know, however, state schools are not without their problems. Large class sizes can make it harder for a dyslexic child to get the attention she needs, and 'streaming' may mean she ends up in a low set, surrounded by disruptive children. Lack of funding means that, in reality, a dyslexic child may not get any extra help, especially if parents don't push for it.

Advice:

- State schools are required to give dyslexic children support – make sure your child gets it!
- Push the school for action on your child's dyslexia: talk to the class teacher, the SENCo, *and* the head teacher.
- Don't let the subject drop: make a fuss if you have to!

Rote learning programmes

Pros:

- Less expensive than private school
- Child can build up a strong work ethic

Cons:

- Rote learning doesn't work well for dyslexic children
- Ongoing cost
- Doesn't follow the National Curriculum
- Child may see it as 'more of the same school stuff' that she hates

Popular in Asia, many brand-name rote learning programmes have now hit UK shores. For a fee, children go to regular classes outside of school, where they're given work books in English or maths. Pupils proceed through the work books, both in class and at home (20–30 minutes of study per day is usually required). The idea is that constant repetition will drill key facts into the child's brain.

Unfortunately, rote learning simply doesn't work well for dyslexic children. Dyslexics learn better in a multi-sensory way (practising facts in lots of different ways, using sight, sound, touch, smell, and taste).

Rote learning, on the other hand, encourages a child to practise facts over and over again in just one way. A dyslexic child probably won't understand the importance or context of what she's supposed to be learning. She won't make connections with previous learning, and the facts won't go into her long-term memory.

What's more, rote learning programmes can lull parents into a false sense of security. You may see your child working away, completing work book after work book, but months later, it becomes apparent she has made hardly any progress.

Advice:

- Rote learning may work for non-dyslexic children, but it doesn't work for dyslexic children.
- Instead, spend half an hour a day with your child, playing dyslexia-friendly learning games (available to download for free from the defeat-dyslexia.com website).

Group dyslexia sessions

Pros:

- Learning tailored to dyslexic children
- Well-resourced
- Often (but not always) run by qualified, specialist teachers

Cons:

- Often expensive
- Not always personalised to your child
- Unregulated – quality may vary
- Might be held at an inconvenient time or location

Regional dyslexia associations (often affiliated to the British Dyslexia Association or Dyslexia Action) run regular sessions for groups of children. These sessions, which can help children to build up strategies to deal with their dyslexia, tend to follow a set programme. The programme is usually well thought out and taught by dyslexia experts.

However, because the programme is very rigid, not all of it will be relevant to your child. Children won't get personalised help. What's more, some sessions are held during the day. This means parents may be asked to pull their child out of school for half a day per week, so the child may fall behind in her lessons. This is far from ideal for children who need more help in school, rather than less.

Advice:

- Group sessions are certainly better than nothing, but most dyslexic children need personalised support as well.
- Sit in on a session beforehand to see how relevant it might be for your child.
- Opt for sessions held in the evenings and on weekends, to avoid pulling your child out of school.

One-to-one tutoring

Pros:

- Less expensive than private school
- Personalised help
- Supportive environment

Cons:

- Ongoing cost
- Unregulated – quality may vary
- Child may see it as 'more of the same school stuff' that she hates

Weekly sessions of one-to-one tutoring from a qualified teacher and/or dyslexia expert can really benefit children – provided the tutor is knowledgeable. For a small fee, a child can get personalised support, to help her to improve her weak areas and build up strategies for the future. Tutors usually offer worksheets and home study materials, as well as detailed marking and feedback. Basically, everything you'd like from school, but might not get!

However, parents should make sure the tutor really is helping their child. Many tutors are not trained teachers, and even teachers don't always know a lot about dyslexia. Because tutors don't follow a particular programme or the National Curriculum, it can be hard to tell if what the tutor is teaching your child is helpful or even correct. This makes it important to track your child's progress closely.

Advice:

- A good local tutor can help a dyslexic child to make rapid progress for a relatively low cost.

- Get recommendations from other parents of dyslexic children, from an Educational Psychologist, or via PATOSS (Professional Association of Teachers of Students with Specific Learning Difficulties).

- Ask to sit in on a tutoring session beforehand, to see how relevant it might be for your child.

- Always ask to see the tutor's DBS check (Disclosure and Barring Service, formerly CRB) and PGCE (Post Graduate Certificate of Education) teaching qualification.

- If your child isn't making progress, find a new tutor!

18.

LOOKING FORWARD

"
'You've got to find your dream and then do it. It could be hard work. Trust me: being a space scientist with dyslexia is hard work.'

— **MAGGIE ADERIN-POCOCK (dyslexic scientist)**

Space scientist and BBC presenter

THERE'S A REASON THE MEDIA IS QUICK TO REDUCE DYSLEXIA TO 'trouble with reading'. The reality is that dyslexia is vast in scope – and that can be a little bit terrifying for parents. However, the hardest part is now over for you, as the parent of a dyslexic child. *You get it.* After reading this book, I hope that you now understand dyslexia: what it is; what it isn't; why your child struggles in some areas and excels in others. This knowledge is power – and it can change how you help your child to learn.

Going forward, you'll now understand the type of support your child needs in order to make good progress. Supporting a dyslexic child isn't hard, as long as you get to grips with his weak areas. By applying the strategies suggested in this book, your child can begin to defeat his demons and embrace the best of his dyslexia.

The route forward for you might involve enlisting the help of a professional like an Educational Psychologist, working closely with the school SENCo, or finding a private tutor. However, for parents who would like to personally take on the challenge of helping their child with his schoolwork, a guiding hand may be needed. With this in mind, I will soon be publishing a series of *Defeat Dyslexia!* field guides for helping your child with English, maths, and more. These guides provide a long-term plan of action for success in school, with games and activities to make learning enjoyable.

Don't want to wait for these books to be published? No problem! Download worksheets and educational games for free at the defeat-dyslexia.com website right now.

When it comes to helping a dyslexic child, there's no fix-it-quick solution, but there is a secret. The secret is a simple one: F-U-N. Yep, that's right. All you need to do is turn schoolwork from a chore into a treat (or, you know, a little bit less of a chore). So don't be afraid to make homework into a game or combine learning with laughing.

Making learning fun again is usually the key to a dyslexic child racing ahead in school. In the past, learning may have been a frustrating or confusing experience for him. But, when his needs are understood and supported, all of that can change.

For parents and children alike, the message is the same: Good luck. Work hard. Have fun.

HOLLY'S DYSLEXIA STORY

W HEN I WAS GROWING UP, I NEVER THOUGHT IT WAS strange that I had to read a paragraph of writing ten times to understand the meaning. I thought everyone 'cheated' at their times tables, quickly adding on the next digit as they recited 'two threes are six, three threes are nine ...' I assumed everyone had a brief moment of panic when they looked at their watch and tried to tell the time.

Of course, I noticed that not everyone got lost constantly; not everyone was forgetful and disorganised; not everyone checked their work obsessively and wrote 20 drafts of an essay, the way I did. When I compared myself with other people in my class, I could see that there was a difference. I didn't know the word 'dyslexic', though, so I used one that I did know: stupid.

On a daily basis, I called myself stupid in my head. I couldn't do the basic maths everyone else could do. (Stupid!) Acting the lead in the school play, I forgot my lines. (Stupid!) I messed up my driving test because I mixed up left and right. (Stupid!)

There was another voice in my head, though; one that told me, *no, you really are clever*. That voice belonged to my mum.

The contradiction made me feel confused (how could I be clever when I made such stupid mistakes?), but my mother's faith in me meant that I never gave up. My mum always bolstered my self-esteem. This, combined with her willingness to work with me at home on times tables, handwriting, spelling, and more, was a big part of the reason I was able to excel at school and go on to university. I did so well academically (as a result of hard work and study strategies that I developed myself) that it never occurred to anyone that I might have a learning difficulty.

Now, of course, I can think back to my childhood and the signs of dyslexia are obvious. Looking at written work from my school days, I notice the tell-tale signs of missing words, no punctuation, easy words misspelled. I now understand why there are so many rubbings-out and 'silly' mistakes in an otherwise-intelligent piece of work.

'Funny' stories from my early life take on new meaning now, as well. When I was in infants' school, I was a great reader. I could read every page in the picture books – or so my teacher thought. Then, one day, the teacher accidentally turned over two pages instead of one. But, instead of reading the page in front of me, I recited what was written on the previous page. It turned out I couldn't read, after all. I'd simply memorised the words to give the impression that I could.

If dyslexia had been more widely understood at the time, someone might have connected the dots and realised that my struggles had their root in an incredibly common learning difference. However, it wasn't until I was in my twenties that I was diagnosed.

This seismic shift of a dyslexia diagnosis entered my life blandly. It was buried in a long list of induction items, as I was shown around the campus on my first day at university: *here's the laundrette; here's the library; here's where you go for a dyslexia screening* ...

I can't quite articulate the reason I chose to go for that dyslexia screening. I didn't know a lot about dyslexia, but I felt subtly pursued by this tricky little word. At an office job I'd held prior to university, I would often find myself making misspellings when I typed phrases into Google. For some reason, these misspellings meant that I was redirected to a web page that asked, *Do you think you might be dyslexic?*

No. No one had ever told me I was dyslexic. But, nonetheless, I kept ending up on that web page.

At university, I still didn't think I was dyslexic. Nonetheless, I chose to take the university's dyslexia screening – on a dusty old computer in the library – as soon as I was able.

At the end of the screening, a message flashed up on the screen: *Congratulations, you are dyslexic!*

(It didn't really say that, but it's how I tend to remember it.)

The computer screening was quick, but getting the official diagnosis took much longer. I had to wait six months to be seen by an Educational Psychologist. Luckily, he was very nice, during what turned out to be a harrowing, humiliating day. Initially, I tried to fudge my way through the assessment. I guessed at answers. I put on my best performance as a confident, able reader – and then I burst into tears.

I was utterly humiliated at having to reveal things about myself that I'd put so much effort into concealing. There was my weak working memory, which made it difficult for me to remember a chain of even three digits. There was my dismal reading comprehension, which required me to read and re-read a passage in order to understand it. All of these things were suddenly under a microscope – and I hated it.

It's little wonder that, after the assessment, I put the Educational Psychologist's report on my dyslexia in a drawer without reading it.

It's a strange contradiction, because I can say wholeheartedly that my dyslexia diagnosis was a huge relief for me. (After all, 'dyslexic' was a much better label than the one I'd been using before: 'stupid'.) And yet that report from the Educational Psychologist haunted me.

In fact, I didn't read it for more than ten years. It wasn't until I started writing this book and my co-author asked to see the report that I finally pulled it out of the drawer. Even after so many years had passed – even after embarking on a successful career helping other dyslexics – reading about my own dyslexia was incredibly hard. I had to read the report in three sittings, taking long breaks to collect myself. I felt very alone.

The dry, dispassionate language of the report made me feel inadequate. That was the problem when I was first diagnosed: I was given the label 'dyslexic', but no one ever really explained to me what it meant. The university gave me a laptop to help with my studies, but offered no guidance on dealing with dyslexia. My family, though they tried to be supportive, didn't know anything about dyslexia. I had a few dyslexic friends, but they were just as clueless about the condition as I was.

For a long time, dyslexia was a part of me, but one which I scarcely understood. I got through university and my postgraduate teacher training the same way I'd got through school: hard work and lots of it. While my non-dyslexic friends could afford to slack off sometimes, I never could: I worked all day, every day, in order to get my BA and PGCE (Postgraduate Certificate in Education). I spent my PGCE year on five hours of sleep a night, working harder and harder and harder to achieve my dream of becoming a teacher.

Dyslexia might have remained an unexamined part of my identity if it weren't for a girl named Chelsea, a friend's daughter who I offered to tutor. Chelsea is bright but dyslexic, and I couldn't help but see myself in her. I passed on to her the strategies for coping with dyslexia that I'd developed over the years, but I wanted to do more for her. So I set about learning everything I could about dyslexia.

I read every book on dyslexia I could lay my hands on. I attended umpteen courses. I tried out myriad learning resources, computer programs, and different teaching approaches, in order to see what worked best. I set out to help Chelsea, but of course, I ended up helping myself as well.

For the first time, I was able to understand why 'I am the way I am'. All those idiosyncrasies of mine, all those weird little habits ... I began to see their root was in my dyslexia. And I began to realise just how many children and adults there are around the world who are struggling with the same things as me.

I wish that, when I'd been diagnosed, someone had sat me down and talked me through dyslexia. I wish I could hop in a time machine, and go back and see that humiliated version of myself who cried during her dyslexia assessment. No, I wish I could go back further. I'd go and see that little girl in infants' school who simply *pretended* she could read. I'd tell her: You are not alone. You are not stupid. Your brain is wired differently, but by working smarter, in ways that suit you, you will be able to fly.

I can't time-travel, but I can communicate that message to dyslexics like me. It's what has led me to specialise in tutoring dyslexic children. It's the reason I've trained to become a dyslexia assessor. It's why I organise free workshops for children, and support groups for parents of dyslexic children. And, of course, it has inspired me to write this book – the book I wish I'd been able to read all those years ago.

Even today, I'm still a slow reader. I still need to obsessively check my work. I still have that brief, blank moment when I look at my watch and try to tell the time. I still mix up left and right when I'm stressed. But I can also see the incredible positives of dyslexia, too.

Like many dyslexic people, I question everything and I'm a very creative problem solver, making new connections and coming up with innovative ideas. I also have great determination to overcome obstacles in my path. I've learned not to believe those who tell me I am not able to do things.

Dyslexics are everywhere, in every walk of life. And I know that we can do anything we set our minds to.

NOW TELL ME YOUR STORY

KEEN TO LEARN EVEN MORE ABOUT DYSLEXIA? MY WEBSITE, **www.defeat-dyslexia.com**, is filled with blog posts, interviews with successful dyslexics, and opportunities to 'Ask the Dyslexia Lady' (that's me!) about any of your concerns. For parents hoping to make homework time more fun, there are also worksheets and games to download for free.

Follow me

Please follow me on Twitter, **@defeat_dyslexia**, or on Tumblr, **defeatdyslexia.tumblr.com**. I'd love to hear from you!

Write a review or tell a friend

This book is independently published, which means that Amazon reviews are incredibly important to its success. If you enjoyed *Defeat Dyslexia!*, please consider writing a review, sending out a tweet, or simply passing this book on to a friend.

APPENDIX

SUGGESTED FURTHER READING

PHONICS-BASED READING BOOKS – COMPREHENSIVE READING PROGRAMMES:

Coleman, Libby, and Nick Ainley. *Yes We Can Read*. Gatehouse Books, 2010. Print.

Cowling, Keda, and Frank Cowling. *Stride Ahead*. Keda Publications, 2001. Print.

PHONICS-BASED READING BOOKS – STORY BOOKS:

Corby, Jill. *Say the Sounds* series. Ladybird Books Ltd. Print.

Donaldson, Julia. *Songbirds* series. OUP Oxford. Print.

Jones, Allan Frewin. *Talisman* series. Hodder Children's Books. Print.

Miskin, Ruth. **Read Write Inc.** series. OUP Oxford. Print.

Ross, Mandy. **Superhero** series. Ladybird Books Ltd. Print.

ON DYSLEXIA AND DYSPRAXIA:

Beaton, Alan. **Dyslexia, Reading and the Brain:** *A Sourcebook of Psychological and Biological Research.* Psychology Press, 2004. Print.

Christmas, Jill. **Hands On Dyspraxia:** *Supporting Children and Young People with Sensory and Motor Learning Challenges.* Speechmark Publishing Ltd, 2009. Print.

Evans, Bruce. **Dyslexia and Vision**. Wiley-Blackwell, 2001. Print.

Hulme, Charles, and Margaret Snowling. **Reading Development and Dyslexia**. Singular Publishing Group, 1994. Print.

Kirby, Amanda, and Sharon Drew. **Guide to Dyspraxia and Developmental Coordination Disorders**. David Fulton Publishers, 2003. Print.

Miles, Tim, and Elaine Miles. **Dyslexia and Mathematics**, *2nd Edition*. Routledge, 2004. Print.

Miles, Tim et al, eds. **Music and Dyslexia:** *A Positive Approach*. Wiley-Blackwell, 2008. Print.

Miles, T.R., and Elaine Miles. *Dyslexia: A Hundred Years On*. Open University Press, 1999. Print.

Talukdar, Afroza. *Dyspraxia/DCD Pocketbook*. Teachers' Pocketbooks, 2012. Print.

Terrell, Colin, and Terri Passenger. *ADHD, Autism, Dyslexia and Dyspraxia (Understanding)*. Family Doctor Publications Ltd, 2006. Print.

Thomson, Patience, and Peter Gilchrist, eds. *Dyslexia: A Multidisciplinary Approach*. Nelson Thornes, 1996. Print.

OTHER LEARNING DIFFICULTIES:

Attwood, Tony. *The Complete Guide to Asperger's Syndrome*. Jessica Kingsley Publishers, 2008. Print.

Hallowell, Edward M., and John J. Ratey. *Driven to Distraction: Recognizing and Coping with Attention Deficit Disorder from Childhood Through Adulthood*. Touchstone, 1995. Print.

APPENDIX

NOTES

THIS BOOK IS NOT DESIGNED TO BE AN ACADEMIC WORK AND much of what it contains comes from my own observations of dyslexic children. However, I also undertook rigorous library research to back up every claim, wherever possible. Of the dozens of books I read, many remain unmentioned, because they contain well-established information about dyslexia. The sources listed in these notes are instances where a particular book proved particularly illuminating. I have also listed sources for all of the quotable dyslexics found within this book's pages.

Introduction

'My greatest asset is my dyslexia': Benjamin Zephaniah quoted in 'The real me at 18: the personal statements of five public figures'. *Guardian*. 7 December 2012.

Chapter 1: Myths and Facts About Dyslexia

one in ten people is dyslexic: Statistic from: The British Dyslexia Association. www.bdadyslexia.org.uk. Web. 17 October 2013.

combination of genetic effects on biochemistry: Information on the genetic basis of dyslexia summarised from: Miles, T.R, and Elaine Miles. *Dyslexia: A Hundred Years On*. Open University Press, 1999. Print.

Chapter 3: Dys-what-ia?: A Quick Guide to Key Terms

abnormal development of how the brain copes with numbers: The definition of dyscalculia paraphrased from: Butterworth, Brian. *The Mathematical Brain*. Macmillan, 1999.

dyscalculia should be applied more broadly: Steve Chinn, in *Dealing with Dyscalculia: Sum Hope* (Souvenir Press Ltd, 2007), argues dyscalculia should be defined as any difficulty with maths.

classed as the same condition: Tim Miles, in *Dyslexia and Mathematics* (Routledge, 2004), cautions that dyslexia and dyscalculia may be better classified as the same syndrome.

Chapter 4: Seeing

'My dyslexia's a weird one': Jamie Oliver quoted in: 'Jamie Oliver, the naked chef, opens up about family life'. *Telegraph*. 25 December 2010.

Information on binocular instability and Meares-Irlen Syndrome summarised from: Evans, Bruce. *Dyslexia and Vision*. Wiley-Blackwell, 2001. Print.

Chapter 5: Reading

'My perseverance and love of reading': Carol W Greider quoted in 'Carol W. Greider - Biographical'. *Nobelprize.org*. Web. 10 May 2013.

Chapter 6: Spelling

'People with dyslexia often': Ari Emanuel quoted in 'Lab School Gala - Speech by Ari Emanuel'. *Youtube.com*. 22 January 2008. Web. 10 May 2013.

Some information gathered from: Critchley, Macdonald. *The Dyslexic Child*. William Heinemann Medical Books, 1970. Print.

Chapter 7: Writing

'I write children's books': Henry Winkler quote from the Yale Center For Dyslexia & Creativity website: 'Henry Winkler, Actor, Producer, Author'. *Dyslexia.yale.edu*. Web. 10 May 2013.

John Irving says that the process: John Irving quoted in: Shaywitz, Sally. *Overcoming Dyslexia: A New and Complete Science-Based Program for Reading Problems at Any Level*. Vintage, 2005.

Chapter 8: Speaking and Listening

'Dyslexia doesn't mean that you're': Keira Knightley quoted in 'Keira Knightley: dyslexia "doesn't mean you're stupid"'. *BBC.co.uk/newsround*. 4 September 2012. Web. 10 May 2013.

Some information on auditory discrimination gathered from: Thomson, Patience, and Peter Gilchrist, eds. *Dyslexia: A Multidisciplinary Approach*. Nelson Thornes, 1996. Print.

Chapter 9: Maths

'I'm very open about my dyslexia': Diane Swonk quote from the Yale Center For Dyslexia & Creativity website: 'Diane Swonk, Economist'. *Dyslexia.yale.edu*. Web. 10 May 2013.

officially recognised by the government in 2001: Dyscalculia was officially recognised by the government in the Department for Education and Skills circular 0512/2001: *Guidance to support pupils with dyslexia and dyscalculia.*

Some information on how dyslexia interacts with maths gathered from: Miles, Tim, and Elaine Miles. *Dyslexia and Mathematics, 2nd Edition*. Routledge, 2004. Print.

Chapter 10: Movement

'a kind of privilege': David Bailey quoted in 'The old Bailey'. *Guardian*. 29 July 2002.

visualise every lap, every gear change: Information on famous athletes with dyslexia summarised from 'Evidence grows that sport is a productive path for dyslexics'. *Independent*. 21 July 2011.

'so horribly difficult': Darcey Bussell quoted in 'Why I can never be a normal mother'. *Daily Mail*. 9 August 2012.

Some information on dyspraxia gathered from: Kirby, Amanda, and Sharon Drew. *Guide to Dyspraxia and Developmental Coordination Disorders*. David Fulton Publishers, 2003. Print.

Additional information gathered from: Christmas, Jill.

Hands On Dyspraxia: Supporting Children and Young People with Sensory and Motor Learning Challenges. Speechmark Publishing Ltd, 2009. Print.

Additional information gathered from: Critchley, Macdonald. *The Dyslexic Child*. William Heinemann Medical Books, 1970. Print.

Chapter 11: Time and Organisation

'I just approach problems differently': John Chambers quoted in 'Overcoming Dyslexia'. *Fortune*. 13 May 2002.

Some information gathered from: Critchley, Macdonald. *The Dyslexic Child*. William Heinemann Medical Books, 1970. Print.

Chapter 12: Music

'Dyslexia made me realise': Richard Rogers quoted in 'Building Civilisation'. *Guardian*. 12 February 2006.

Some information on how dyslexia interacts with musical learning gathered from: Miles, Tim et al, eds. *Music and Dyslexia: A Positive Approach*. Wiley-Blackwell, 2008. Print.

Chapter 13: Foreign Languages

'My dyslexia and my challenges': Ann Bancroft quote from the Yale Center For Dyslexia & Creativity website: 'Ann Bancroft, Teacher & Explorer'. *Dyslexia.yale.edu*. Web. 10 May 2013.

Some information on how dyslexia interacts with foreign languages gathered from: Miles, T.R., and Elaine Miles. *Dyslexia: A Hundred Years On*. Open University Press, 1999. Print.

Additional information from: The British Dyslexia Association. www.bdadyslexia.org.uk. Web. 17 October 2013.

Chapter 14: Problem Solving

'I don't think of dyslexia as a deficiency': William Dreyer quoted in 'Overcoming Dyslexia'. *Fortune*. 13 May 2002.

look beyond pre-conceived ideas: Jack Horner's perspective on dyslexia gathered from 'Dyslexia and Imagination: An Interview with Palaeontologist Jack Horner'. *Youtube.com*. Web. 29 September 2012.

A Cass Business School study: Study conducted by Julie Logan. For more information, see: 'Dyslexic Entrepreneurs: The Incidence; Their Coping Strategies and Their Business Skills'. Wiley InterScience, 2009. Web.

'more intuitive': Richard Branson quoted in Branson, Richard. *Losing My Virginity: The Autobiography*. Crown Business, 1998. Print.

Some information on visuo-spatial awareness gathered

from: Brunswick, Nicola and Neil G. Martin (2009). *Dyslexia and visuospatial ability: is there a causal link?* In: *The Dyslexia Handbook 2009/10*. Brunswick, Nicola, ed. British Dyslexia Association, Bracknell.

Chapter 15: Co-occurring Conditions

'The really social people': Temple Grandin quoted in Grandin, Temple. *Thinking In Pictures, 2nd Edition*. Bloomsbury, 2006. Print.

'think laterally in the comedic sense': Rory Bremner quoted in 'My "butterfly" brain is a blessing and a curse'. *Express*. 7 June 2011.

Information on ADHD summarised from: Hallowell, Edward M., and John J. Ratey. *Driven to Distraction: Recognizing and Coping with Attention Deficit Disorder from Childhood Through Adulthood*. Touchstone, 1995. Print.

Chapter 18: Looking Forward

'You've got to find your dream': Maggie Aderin-Pocock quoted in 'At home: Maggie Aderin-Pocock'. *Financial Times*. 19 October 2012.

APPENDIX

ACKNOWLEDGEMENTS

A BIG THANK YOU TO EVERYONE WHO HELPED BRING THIS BOOK to life:

Jo Ciriani provided copyediting expertise.

Mary-Lynne Michaud offered invaluable proofreading.

Nicky Wilkins gave a thoughtful perspective on coaching dyspraxic children.

Louise Scrivener provided insights into speech and language therapy.

Michelle van Rooyen offered clarity on occupational therapy.

Last but not least, Chelsea Ainsworth is the reason I started my journey of discovery into dyslexia.

Thank you as well to all the switched-on parents who read early versions of this book and offered suggestions for improvement.

APPENDIX

GLOSSARY OF TERMS

> **Note:**
> These definitions have been simplified, for brevity and ease of understanding.

AD(H)D (Attention Deficit (and Hyperactivity) Disorder)

AD(H)D is a condition characterised by impulsivity and distractibility. It can present with or without the restlessness of hyperactivity.

ASD (Autism Spectrum Disorder)

ASD is a condition characterised by a very literal worldview, intense interest in a particular subject, trouble understanding social cues, and (sometimes) emotional meltdowns. Autism exists on a spectrum: children with severe or 'classic' autism may also have obvious problems with speech and movement; children with high-functioning autism may have mild autism traits that are less obvious.

Asperger's Syndrome

Asperger's Syndrome is another term for the high-functioning form of ASD.

Assess, Plan, Do, Review

Assess, Plan, Do, Review is an action plan framework for a child's learning, drawn up by the school. It will typically list three or four short-term targets, focusing on the core areas of communication, literacy, maths, and behaviour. (Formerly, it was called an Individual Education Plan or IEP.)

Auditory discrimination

Auditory discrimination describes how a child's brain processes what she hears. If she has poor auditory discrimination abilities, this makes it harder for her to process the difference between similar sounds, such as /θ/ (*thuh*, as in 'think') and /f/ (*fuh*, as in 'find').

Binocular instability

Binocular instability is a vision-related condition where the eyes don't work together as a team. This can make it more difficult to re-align the eyes on each new sentence while reading.

Clinical Psychologist

Clinical Psychologists work within the healthcare profession to assess and support people with mental health conditions, including ASD and ADHD.

DBS (Disclosure and Barring Service)

The DBS checks a person's criminal record. A DBS check is required for adults who work with children. (Formerly, it was called a Criminal Records Bureau or CRB check.)

DCD (Developmental Coordination Disorder)

DCD is an overarching term for motor-based difficulties, including dyspraxia. However, the two terms are often merged, with 'dyspraxia' commonly used to describe both conditions.

Dyscalculia

Dyscalculia is a condition characterised by very poor number sense, often 'number blindness' (e.g. an inability to look at two numbers and tell which one is bigger).

Dyslexia

Dyslexia is a condition characterised by difficulties with reading, writing, and spelling, as well as problems with phonological awareness, processing speed, working memory, and rapid naming.

Dyspraxia

Dyspraxia primarily affects a child's coordination. Messages about how to move the body may not be correctly transmitted or received by the brain, leading to impaired gross motor skills (walking, sports, etc.) or fine motor skills (handwriting, cutting, etc.). (See also: DCD.)

Educational Psychologist

Educational Psychologists assess and advise on support for children and young people who are experiencing learning difficulties, including dyslexia and dyscalculia.

EHC (Education, Health, and Care) plan

An EHC plan is an action plan for a child, drawn up by the local authority, if she is considered severely at risk and/or she has complex co-occurring difficulties (in addition to dyslexia). (Formerly, it was called a Statement of Special Educational Needs.)

IEP (Individual Education Plan)

IEPs have been replaced by Assess, Plan, Do, Review.

Meares-Irlen Syndrome

Meares-Irlen Syndrome is a condition where visual distortion is experienced when reading under conventional 'white' light (often called page glare). A solution to this problem lies in looking at text through coloured glasses or overlays.

Motor planning

Motor planning is the term for carrying out a series of physical actions in order.

Multi-sensory learning

Multi-sensory learning is an educational approach that uses two or more of the senses (sight, smell, taste, touch, hearing) at the same time to help children to memorise facts and master new skills.

Occupational Therapist

Occupational Therapists assess and support people who have physical problems in a range of areas, such as difficulties with gross motor skills (walking, sports, etc.) or fine motor skills (handwriting, cutting, etc.). This includes individuals with dyspraxia.

Opaque language

An opaque or non-transparent language is one that doesn't follow a regular, consistent set of rules. Languages vary in their spelling complexity, but examples of opaque languages include English, French, Danish, and Portuguese.

Oral motor dyspraxia

Oral motor dyspraxia is another term for verbal dyspraxia.

PATOSS

PATOSS is the Professional Association of Teachers of Students with Specific Learning Difficulties. This organisation includes a register of tutors who specialise in dyslexia.

Phonetic spelling

Phonetic spelling is when you spell a word the way you say it – e.g. 'said' is spelled as *sed* and 'graph' is spelled as *graf*.

Phonics

Phonics is a method of teaching children to read that involves decoding the words on the page by 'sounding out' each separate speech sound.

Phonological awareness

Phonological awareness is an understanding of all the speech sounds that make up the English language and an ability to play around with them. For example, good phonological awareness makes it possible to identify rhyming words and find words that begin with the same sound.

Rapid naming

Rapid naming (or rapid automatised naming) is the ability to quickly say the name of an object when it's presented to you.

Rote learning

Rote learning is an educational approach that involves repeating facts over and over again in the same way in order to memorise them.

SENCo (Special Educational Needs Coordinator)

A SENCo works within a school or college to oversee provisions for children with special educational needs, including dyslexia.

SpLD (Specific Learning Difficulties)

SpLD is an umbrella term that refers to dyslexia, dyspraxia, dyscalculia, and sometimes ADHD. These learning difficulties are *specific*, because they only affect certain areas of learning, as opposed to generalised learning difficulties, such as Down's syndrome.

Specialist Assessor

In the dyslexia field, Specialist Assessors are teachers who hold an advanced qualification which means they can carry out official diagnostic screenings for dyslexia.

Statement of Special Educational Needs

Statements of Special Educational Needs have been replaced by EHC plans.

Transparent language

A transparent language is one that follows a regular,

consistent set of rules. Examples of transparent languages include Spanish, Finnish, Greek, and Italian.

Verbal dyspraxia

Verbal dyspraxia (or oral motor dyspraxia) is a type of dyspraxia where a person has trouble coordinating the muscles in her face, mouth, and tongue, making it difficult to chew cleanly or speak clearly.

Visual distortion

Visual distortion occurs in reading, when the words on the page appear to move, blur, or otherwise distort. This condition may be caused by binocular instability or Meares-Irlen Syndrome.

Visuo-spatial awareness

Visuo-spatial awareness determines how good your visual perception is of the spatial relationships of objects. Enhanced visuo-spatial awareness is sometimes described as being able to imagine objects in 3D.

Working memory

Working memory is how we keep track of information, via the short-term memory store. It allows us to remember several pieces of information at once, and also manipulate this information (draw conclusions, solve problems, make connections, etc.).

INDEX